North Atlantic Studies

Local Organisation, Cultural and National Integration in the No.

Poul B. Møller & Susanne Dybbroe, editors

Contents

Contents of next Vol.
The forthcoming vol. 3.2, spring 1992, will contain articles by the following authors: Dona Lee Davis: "Most of us will have to leave; maybe some can stay behind..." Mark Nuttall: "Crofters, incomers and heritage: past and present in a Scottish Highland community." Poul B. Møller: "Images of Greenland in theory and political discourse." Asle Høgmo: "The future of north Norwegian local communities." Finnur Magnússon: "Trade unions and local identity in Iceland." Peter I. Crawford: "Friends and foes, cosmopolitans and strangers: hybridisation in Europe – the Welsh case." Jørgen Ole Bærenholdt: "Village life in the North Atlantic: between local and global conditions of existence."

VOL. 3 · NO. 1 · AARHUS 1991

North Atlantic Studies

Publishers:
SNAI-North Atlantic Publications. Distribution in cooperation with *Aarhus University Press (Aarhus Universitetsforlag),* Aarhus University, DK 8000 Aarhus C, Denmark.

Editors:
Editorial board:
Susanne Dybbroe *(Department of Social Anthropology, Aarhus University);* Poul B. Møller *(Center for North Atlantic Studies, Aarhus University);* Elisabeth Vestergaard *(Center for North Atlantic Studies, Aarhus University);* Torben A. Vestergaard *(Department of Social Anthropology, Aarhus University);* Vagn Wåhlin *(Department of History, Aarhus University).*

Advisory Board:
Claus Andreasen *(Ilisimatusarfik, University of Greenland, Nuuk);* Simun V. Arge *(Føroya Fornminnissavn/The Faroe National Museum, Tórshavn, The Faroe Islands);* Dorete Bloch, *(Føroya Náttúrugripasavn/Museum of Natural History, Tórshavn);* Otto Blehr *(Department of Anthropology, University of Stockholm);* Harald Eidheim *(Department of Social Anthropology, Oslo University, Norway);* Michal Fortescue *(Department of Eskimology, University of Copenhagen, Denmark);* Kirsten Hastrup (Dept. of Social Antrhopology, University of Copenhagen); Jóan Pauli Joensen *(Frøðskaparsetur Føroya/ The Faroe University, Tórshavn);* Orvar Löfgren *(Department of Ethnology, University of Lund, Sweden);* Tinna Møbjerg *(Department of Archaeology, Aarhus University, Denmark);* Bertel Møhl *(Department of Biology, Aarhus University);* Gísli Pálsson *(Faculty of Social Science, University of Iceland,, Reykjavík);* Robert Petersen *(Ilisimatusarfik/ University of Greenland, Nuuk);* Povl Simonsen *(Department of Archaeology, University of Tromsø, Norway);* Vilhjálmur Ö. Vilhjálmsson *(Department of Medieval Archaeology, Aarhus University);* Jonathan Wylie *(Massachusett Institute of Technology, USA).*

CNS Executive Committee:
Susanne Dybbroe, Torben A. Vestergaard, Vagn Wåhlin.

Address:
SNAI-North Atlantic Publications, *Center for Nordatlantiske Studier,* Aarhus Universitet, Finlandsgade 26, DK 8200 Aarhus N, Denmark.
Phone: (45)-86-16 52 44, telefax: (45)-86-10 82 28.
Bank: Den Danske Bank, Universitetspark Afdl., Langelandsgade 177, DK 8200, Aarhus, Denmark.

Subscription:
Aarhus University Press (Aarhus Universitetsforlag), Aarhus University, DK 8000 Aarhus C, Denmark. Phone: -86-19 70 33.
Postal Account: 7 41 69 54.
Subscription price, for single issues D.Kr. 80 + postage + VAT.
Booksellers price: 120 D.Kr. + VAT + postage.
By order of 10 or more copies directly from Aarhus University Press special offer: 100 D.Kr. (+ postage + VAT) pr. copy.

Financial support:
SNAI-North Atlantic Publications is a non-profit private foundation. The editors express their sincere thanks for financial support to this publication from *the foundations mentioned in the Introduction.*

Manuscripts:
North Atlantic Studies takes no responsibility for unrequested manuscripts. All manuscripts will be submitted to evaluation by two scholars selected according to the subject of the article – the examiners will be anonymous to the author.
Manuscripts should be submitted in duplicate including a one-page summary. Double space all text on quarto or A-4 paper using only one side of the page. Max. 25 pages à 2000 characters. If at all possible manuscripts should be accompanied by a disc version in IBM or Machintosh WordPerfect. Submit a short (max. 60 words) presentation of the author.
Figures and tables should be submitted ready for reproduction.

Advertising:
Advertisments should be submitted ready for reproduction.
Price: a half page, D.Kr. 750, full page D.Kr. 1.500.

Print and lay-out:
Werks Offset, Aarhus

ISBN: 87-983424-8-7
ISSN: 0905-2984

Cover ill.:
Sami Shaman's drum depicted in Friis: *Lappisk mytologi* (1871).

Editorial

Poul B. Møller & Susanne Dybbroe

In the global political and economic realities of today, *localism* tend to be seen as archaic, a vestige of traditionalism, or in terms of its disruptive effects on the national (state) unity of which the community or region forms part. Obvious examples of this are contexts where the richer part of a nation state aspires to independence, and contexts of political resistance by peripheral groups, acting in terms of the *right to self-determination* of their respective regions.

Defined as a consciousness of *local belonging*, localism may alternatively be seen to reflect a condition of life pertinent to all corners of the globe, which is that the local community provides the primary relations basic to the acquiring of culture. Hence locality – as an empirically shifting frame of reference – constitutes a point of orientation for individuals and groups in their relationships to the encompassing society. In this sense belonging to localised communities may become an argument for cultural differentiation in its own right, i. e. that identity is directly coupled to time and place of origin.

Communities also exist, however, which are of a less tangible kind, such as ethnic or national communities. In this extended meaning of the term, *community* in the sense of 'collectivity' or 'collective identity' is mediated by factors of other kinds than locality – and what inheres in the facts of social proximity and sharing of physical space – integrating individuals and groups in the society. – Religion and ethnicity are examples of such 'collectivities' to which membership can be defined in terms of categorial relations reaching across locality. As such, they may never form symbolically 'cohesive', i. e. bounded, communities. Whether or not these factors turn out to be generative of community feeling and action, and how they relate to the local/national nexus, is a matter of historical contingency. – The hierarchical relations between the local and national level of organisation and the relations between horisontal segments of society, i.e. ethnic groups or local communities, articulate in ways so as to attribute differential meaning and inspire variable symbolic importance to levels of community.

The *3rd North Atlantic Studies Conference* in Aarhus, October 20-23, 1990, with the title: *Local Organisation, Cultural Identity and National Integration in the North Atlantic*, addressed this theme. The conference papers collected in the present volume seem to indicate a connection between progressive centralisation – corresponding with increased homogeneity of culture at the national level – and a concomitant relative heterogenisation of peripheral regions and minority culture in political terms, expressed through the assertion of difference – of local, regional, ethnic etc. identities. This "heterogenisation" may be defined in cultural terms as *differentiation* or in structural terms as expressing a *relative distancing* from the centres of power. The factors giving form and content to these movements seem to reflect institutional arrangements made by the centres in an effort to integrate peripheral communities. In other words, expressions of 'localism' are linked to the manner and structure of integration in the social system or society in question. This puts focus on public *institutions* as integrating mechanisms and possible arenas of struggle for control. Paraphrasing Jenkins (this vol.), comparing Northern Irish and Welsh nationalism, 'the character of nationalist movements is inextricably bound up with the processes of modern state formation.'

The focus on structures and relations of incorporation or integration is a general theme uniting the present collection of articles, although this observation alone does not do justice to the breadth of perspectives taken:

A basic question relates to the way locality is perceived – in an actual, empirical, as well as in a theoretical sense. Empirically, what does it mean to "be from" a place? – And on the other hand, what sociological importance may be attributed to locality? The article by *Susanne Dybbroe* explores what seems a central question, namely the relation between 'place' and 'social organisation' and the terms of influence of these two factors on identity. In other words, how is 'community', the sense of belonging and cultural identity, related to 'local organisation', and what are the implications with respect to cultural integration at the level of the Greenlandic nation. An important question relates to the cultural space in which locality is given meaning, since this can be assumed to condition its symbolic importance at the local level and in a national setting.

Louis-Jacques Dorais discusses the relation between language and identity among contemporary Canadian Inuit. The perspective taken is a socio-linguistic analysis of the institutional integration of Inuit in Canadian society and the differential significance of Inuktitut at the national resp. community level, conditioned by the relations of participation of Inuit in Canadian society. The conditions of modern life forces a situation upon the Inuit where two languages are needed, even locally. However, Inuktitut continues to be the language spoken at the level of community, reflecting semantic categories and a structure of meaning that has nothing to do with mainstream Canadian concepts. At the national level, however, Inuktitut is mainly treated as a symbol with primarily political importance.

In the analysis of 'discourses of Sami self-awareness', *Vigdis Stordahl* demonstrates that processes of change after the Second World War have simultaneously drawn the Sami into the Norwegian State *and* pulled the Sami community together as a separate nation through a process of what is called 'ethnic incorporation'. The article in an important sense highlights the 'fact' that, as also stressed by Dorais, identity is not made up by objective characteristics. Rather, Saminess is in a process of perpetual formation and negotiation. A point which is noted by the author is that the closer relation between the ethnic groups in Norway have, on the one hand, threatened Sami identity, yet – by way of the very same institutions mediating this threat, such as education, the media, occupational changes – created a new opportunity situation, which is part of the present day realities of being Sami and which is being utilised for the purpose of defining a modern Sami self-awareness.

Northern Ireland and Wales are both arenas of nationalist struggle against the British State. The two 'nationalisms' however, manifest their aims in strikingly different ways. Whereas violence has for the last decades been the primary tool of the Northern Irish struggle, the legitimate means to achieve the goals of the Welsh have been constitutional democratic politics and a limited degree of direct action and protest. Conversely, the language factor is of no political significance in Northern Ireland, where Irish is no longer spoken, whereas language is central in Wales, where the salience of Welsh in the public domain has been notably increasing over the last decades. Besides contributing to an understanding of the differences in emphasis of the nationalist movements of Northern Ireland and Wales, *Richard Jenkins* questions the analytical significance of established sociological notions of 'nationalism'.

The article by *Ivar Bjørklund* deals with the conflict between opposed paradigms of fisheries management systems, – the common property theory held by the Norwegian State and the traditional tenure system of the coastal Sami population in a north Norwegian fiord, implying a practice of property in common. The perspective of the State authorities have prevented them, over the years, from recognizing the existence of a Sami tenure system, regulating access to fishery resources by a differential system of rights held in common and individual usufruct rights, as well as by a system of practical knowledge reducing outside encroaching on what was considered local 'exclusive' rights. The State fisheries management regime, however, by not limiting the access of large-scale fisheries to Sami fishing grounds, has caused a depletion of fishery resources and hence threatened the survival of local fisheries.

Søren Thuesen's article concerns the significance of associations in the life of two local comunities in West Greenland. The author traces the origin and development of different kinds of association and discusses their role in structuring community life vis-à-vis more formal societal structures. The perspective is on intra- and inter-ethnic symbolic interaction in colonial Greenland, that is, between Greenlanders resp. Greenlanders and Danes in a context of colonial inter-ethnic hierarchy. It is argued that local associations since about the turn of the century have furthered the development of a national Greenlandic identity.

The Faroe Islands considered as a semi-autonomous political system closely tied to the Danish State, is analysed by *Jógvan Mørkøre* focusing on the structural features characterising Faroese party politics as compared to the parliamentary traditions of the Nordic countries. A central feature of the Nordic political party system is its linkage to the class structure, which makes the left/right dichotomy – left for socialism, right for conservatism – a salient characteristic of parliamentary politics. The opposition operates so as to position political parties according to "class-principles", i.e. in matters of economy and the nation. Mørkøre demonstrates, adopting a historical perspective in the elaboration of party developments and -positions before and after the Second World War, how Faroese political parties, described in terms of Nordic left/right positions, relate to issues of traditional left/right concern: economic policy and the national question.

We wish to thank *Aarhus Universitets Forskningsfond* for contributing the economic means to the publication.

Local Organisation and Cultural Identity in Greenland in a National Perspective

Susanne Dybbroe

ABSTRACT

Important contributions have been made to understand the function of locality in the construction of cultural identity. Focus has variously been directed at the role of place and the role of aspects of social organisation in creating a symbolic bond between members of local communities. The article discusses contextual meanings of locality in Greenland and sketches possible implications for the symbolic integration of locality and nation. Proceeding by way of an outline of the importance of 'place' underlying the social organisation of communities in the traditional-contact Inuit society, it is concluded that the symbolic importance of local communities is a function of their integration in the wider social structure[1].

A number of recent ethnographic studies have been concerned with the role of local organisation in constructing cultural identity. Whether the focus is on locality as such, (places and their use, Nuttall 1991) or on types of social relationships (forms of close social association, Cohen 1982a and b), the concern is with the *sense of belonging* acquired by members of a local community. In the meaning of Cohen, this identity is an expression of the *symbolic construction of community*, effected in the contexts of close social interaction, where 'culture' is acquired (Cohen 1985: 15).

The studies shed important light on the symbolic importance of particular kinds of local organisation with respect to the positioning of individuals in time and space. The focus of the two authors differs. Both, however, contribute to a common theoretical project, which is to understand the identity evolving in local communities in terms of the understanding by a group of "actors" of what it means to "belong". Characteristic of this approach is a reliance on the cultural interpretation of interaction. It is assumed that identity is constructed in discourse (Cohen 1982 and 1987). Having become aware of one's identity or culture by way of interaction with some "other", value is attributed to this culture and to the other culture confronting it[2].

Cohen, defining this project as I see it, has an explicit sociological objective in trying to account for the relation between part and whole – individual/ collective in the context of social interaction, community/society at a more abstract level. To Cohen there is no doubt that 'community', apart from its sociological reference, is also a *rhetoric*. As such local identity is a symbolic construction, where (the fact of) peripherality in the objective world informs the sense of belonging and identity. Peripherality is not just a political reality, but becomes a 'state of mind'.

In Cohen's analysis of Whalsay community identification the emphasis is on the processes "which associate the individual to the community through the medium of the 'sections' to which he may regard himself, or may be regarded by others, as belonging" (Cohen 1982b: 22). An important aspect of these consists in the rationalisation or "derandomization" of kinds of social relationships which are particularly legitimate as means of access to being 'Whalsa', yet do not compromise their respective sectional interests:

> "These structures /of kinship, neighbourhood and fishing crew (SD)/ are being transformed from real frameworks for social organisation and action into idioms for legitimating association and for creating a *rhetoric of historical and cultural continuity* to mask the substantial change evident in Whalsay social life.
> *When people thus identify themselves as belonging to Whalsay they merge the primacy of their immediate kinship and neighbouring associations with the community as a whole.* They merge a tradition, a folk history, with the present. They thus make time and place a vocabulary which is so fluid that it can serve and mask the conflicting demands of the different sections to which they belong." (Cohen 1982b: 21, emphasis added.)

Nuttall in his description of landscape as "memoryscape" emphasises a similar dimension in the construction of local identity in Kangersuatsiaq (in the municipality of Upernavik, Northwest Greenland), vis. that through the fusion of individual and collective memory in places and place names a sense of belonging is attained, which demarcates the local community from other communities:

> *"My concern ...is with landscape as memoryscape... memoryscape is constructed with people's mental images of the environment, with particular emphasis on places as remembered places."*

> *"The area utilized by an individual hunter is part of the community hunting area and, by virtue of belonging to the community, the places a hunter frequents are stamped with indelible marks denoting community. These marks are not visible, but are manifest in place names, in memories of hunting and of past events. All give a sense of a bounded locality distinct from the memoryscape of neighbouring communities."* (Nuttall 1991: 3, emphasis added)

These observations in an important sense focus on an aspect of practice, by the way in which the transversion of physical space by members continually reassure individual and group relations to the land and recreate community bonds. In writing an ethnography of place, however, Nuttall does not consider the *structural* terms of identity formation. In his description of place naming Nuttall traces with great insight and subtlety the cultural "incorporation" of territory, i.e. the construction of locality. *This construction operates through* individuals using the land and in this process applying community knowledge of the environment, and *at the same time reflects back upon them*, in turn incorporating them through their individual experiences of belonging to locality that is effected in the process. In another sense, therefore, we are left with a question concerning the sociological reference of practice. The past and the present seems fused in a way which clouds the context of practice, which is always located in a material and symbolic space comprising other practices as well as (and therefore) limitations (Bourdieu 1977; Paine 1974). After all, values are not merely reflected on people but are either taken in or rejected. They are continually created and maybe fought over in social interaction. The context of this interaction extends beyond the local community into a cultural space where *boundaries are made aware* (Cohen 1982a). It is in this sense that the conjuncture of structure and history is important. Nuttall further makes an interesting point:

> *"...landscape and...natural environment...is the physical expression of Kangersuatsiaq and gives a sense of locality important for social continuity and identity. Subsistence activities take place in a specific environment that forms part of a larger system of memory, thought and existence. The landscape is rich in human close association, 'invested with significance in personal or family history'. Recognition of this can increase our understanding of modern Greenland and inform debates about identity. While the local landscape is an expression of community, the emphasis on a national Greenlandic identity obviates recognition of this."* (Nuttall 1991: 16, emphasis added)

I understand this to imply, and with that I agree, that since local identity mediates national identity (Nuttall 1991: 1), a misrecognition or even nonacceptance of local diversity by those in power in Greenland, may compromise the achievement of a common national identity. The issue has of course a history in Greenland, which is to a large degree colonial. The development of heterogeneity in Greenland today can to a large degree be explained by reference to modernisation policies and the resulting industrialised and centralised society. This process has created peripheries both of a national kind – vis. the districts of Thule, East Greenland (Ittoqqortoormiit and Tasiilaq) and Upernavik – and of a regional kind, to which belong most of the smaller settlements along the west coast based on hunting and fishing. Important implications of this are the creation of structural and cultural differences. The question of locality and its role in the construction of identity on a national scale must therefore be posed in another way. The problem is not just one of nonrecognition of local differences. Even positive recognition would not change the fact that, according to my view, identity is not constructed in relations of incorporation only but rather in relations of transaction *and* incorporation. This implies that for any analysis of locality's contribution to nationality to take place, we have to identify important relations between the two levels.

If the emphasis on national Greenlandic identity obviates recognition of local particularities, the question is how and under what circumstances did this come about? How is it expressed? Why cannnot the two levels of community adherence coexist – *if* they cannot? – And not least, how do we go about studying it, identifying the constitutent problematiques?

Since local communities form part of larger state structures, it may be asked, whether it is locality as such or rather the relation between local communities and more encompassing *levels of organisation* that render to locality a more or less pronounced role in the construction of identity. The answer is partly given by reference to the function of locality in creating a sense of belonging in individuals and groups. But only partly. – For instance, as the local community in Greenland – or elsewhere – is not a homogeneous unit whose members entertain invariant worldviews, locality does not mean the same to everybody. Neither can the representation of nation locally be expected to be the same to everybody. Hence the aspect of *community* that represents the local level in anyone context at the national level is likely to be variable also. – Adherence to locality as such cannot, therefore, be attributed a single causal function. The fact that cultural identity is formed in particular contexts, local organisation being one of them, does not immediately tell us *by what processes* this is effected. An important question relates to the *cultural space* in which locality is given meaning, since this can be assumed to condition its symbolic importance at the local level and in a national setting.

Scope of the present article

A discussion of the factors constitutive of various levels of 'community' and of the terms in which culture and community are represented at the local resp. national level, may help clarify the nature of the symbolic relation between locality and nation in Greenland today. The treatment of the subject is premised on the assumption that, in the first place, the symbolic and material world are constitutive of each other and that, in the second place, identity is constructed in social discourse, at the level of social relations operating around relations of difference (Bourdieu 1986) and boundary (Barth 1969; Cohen 1982a and 1987) within an overall society characterized by differential control of symbolic production (Bourdieu 1986; Williams 1972; also Dybbroe 1990a).

To discuss constitutive factors of community, I will adopt a comparative approach and first address the issue of social structure and territoriality with reference to traditional (pre- and contact- [3]) Inuit society, in connection with which this subject has been treated in great detail. This will be followed by a description of patterns of population and settlement today. The purpose is to try to identify structural principles of localisation (local identification) of communities as a frame of reference for discussing locality as a source of identity in a modern Greenlandic context. It is assumed that the degree and kind of structural integration of levels of community and ways of life has a bearing on perceptions of locality (local community identification). By looking at the terms in which culture and community are couched at various levels of discourse, I will try to identify "attitudes" of adherence to local communities, positive as well as negative. This part will include for instance considerations of the distribution of "cultural knowledge", communication competence etc. to account for differences in symbolic control and hence importance of locality in the construction of identity as well as the possibility of incorporating a local perspective in the construction of symbols of national cohesion.

Adherence to local community: nomadic and settled

Legend: love for the home area
A well known legend in Greenland tells about a great hunter from Aluk in East Greenland, who would never leave the place, where he was born[4]. When his covillagers left on hunting trips, he stayed behind with his family (and never lacked means of subsistence, it is noted). In midsummer, it is told, he would get up every day to watch the sun, as it rose over the sea.

While his son grew up, the boy often longed to follow his age mates on their travel. As a grewn man he finally succeeded in persuading his father to go north and see new country. The summer wore on, however, and the old hunter's increasing homesickness forced the family to turn back home. The story tells further that in the morning after the return to Aluk, the old hunter got up early to watch the sun rise. And so great was his happiness at this familiar sight that his heart burst. He was found by his son, lying dead on the ground, facing the sun. After this event the son himself never left Aluk again (Rasmussen 1924)[5].

The origin of this story is unknown to me, except for the fact that it is part of a collection of tales and traditions, most of which were recorded by Knud Rasmussen during the Literary Greenland Expedition, 1902-04. It is sometimes referred to as an example of Greenlanders' love of their home area or feeling for nature (Arima 1976; Schultz-Lorentzen 1928: 256). It seems there would be a number of questions throwing doubt on the general validity of this interpretation. I will list a couple of suggestions:

1. We are told that *the old hunter's behaviour is unusual*. The reason can be inferred, which is, that the viability of the traditional economy was based on a yearly nomadic round in the group territory. In Greenland interspersed with longer, often year long, hunting trips undertaken by single households, during which the households might stay over the winter in some other than the habitual winter settlement (Rink 1875; Bobé 1937). In other words, noone else stayed in the home area because they could not bear to leave it.

2. Yet, *the old man is called a 'great hunter'*. It is usually assumed that the status of *piniartorsuaq*, 'great hunter', was one of considerable prestige (Riches 1982). In Greenland a *piniartorsuaq* would probably be a head of household, *ittoq*, a position which was coupled with a responsibility to take an active part in community matters (Rink 1875 talks about the head of household who, owning the *umiaq*, would have a position equivalent to the *umialiit* (boat owners) of Point Barrow (p. 25) and the responsibilities going with it). At any rate, it seems a bit unlikely that a great hunter was judged only on the basis of his hunting skills. A term such as this must have implied also a man of respect, somebody to whom others listened, and someone whom covillagers counted upon. For this recognition to be of practical consequence, he would have to take part in community activities. Even if "the community" as such is often related to the winter settlement and not to the period of dispersion during summer, it seems unlikely that a *piniartorsuaq* could let himself be carried away by a romance with nature and refrain from participation in summer activities, which included also social gatherings of importance to the winter settlement. – Summer hunting trips meant contact with groups from contiguous settlement areas or

even from regions farther away. Households would not every year stay in the settlement region but would at least occasionally during its life cycle take part in the large regional summer camps, the *aasiviit* (sing. *aasivik*), which were important occasions for the staging of solutions to matters of local judicial concern (Møller and Dybbroe 1981, chp. 3). – In other words, participation in community matters is likely to have demanded more than strictly local interaction[7].

3. Legends often tell about people behaving in opposition to "ordinary" conduct. As noted by writers on oral tradition, such tales among the Inuit may be of even considerable age (Arima 1976). Being an epic tale, however, this legend is probably of post-colonial origin[8], and as such may contain reference to a real occurrance. In the case of Greenland this explains why, in the first place, there can even be talk about staying in the same place year-round. Colonialism disturbed the traditional economic order and, for one thing, wrought havoc to the pattern of year-round and trans-regional movements of groups. In fact, the fact of mobility was *the* issue, with which the missionaries and merchants had to grapple and which they did not solve until the first quarter to a half of the 19th century (Møller & Dybbroe, ibid. chpt. 5; Svejstrup & Dalgaard 1945). – Only around the Moravian missions in South Greenland (which were supposed to have stopped the north-migrating East Greenlanders as early as around the middle of the 18th century (Gulløv 1986)) was sedentarisation achieved earlier.

4. Generally in Greenland from about the middle of the 19th century the pattern of settlement had changed. The Greenlanders, previously semimobile hunters and gatherers, were now settled reasonably permanent during the greater part of the year[9].

An alternative interpretation of the tale may be that it relates a *conflict between nomadism and sedentarism* experienced in the early history of sedentarisation. In pre- and early colonial Greenland mobility was inimicable to the survival of the community. *Under the impact of colonialism, not only were all kinds of blockades to nomadism established, the structures of authority were also definitively altered*: the shaman's moral and intellectual credibility was questioned, as he was even physically attacked by missionaries; occasions for the staging of a community ethos such as religious festivals or other larger gatherings (*aasiviit*, as mentioned) were directly interfered with or otherwise sought controlled by measures of a more indirect kind; also intraregional mobility was stopped, exemplified in the yearly nomadic round (in which the able men had an important say); relations of sharing, so deeply ingrained in indigenous Inuit sociality, were controlled by indirect means; etc. – Consequently, traditional authority crumbled, hunting was specialised and outward directed for the consumption by others than community members, relations of sharing weakened and so did

the original idea of *community*; relations between local communities were cut off; etc. etc. – Maybe a great hunter in particular would see through all this and refuse to leave home, when it was no longer imperative (– he provided well for his family, as the story tells us).

Reconstruction: the sociological importance of territory

There is no direct way of knowing, what locality meant to the old Greenlanders[10]. However, certain general ideas may be established by way of reconstruction or inferred by widening the focus to include comparative evidence from other parts of the Arctic in historic and present light.

Before and around the time of colonisation, the geographical organisation in Greenland was based on *miut*-groups, consisting of aggregates of households, defined by their traditional use of a particular area of land. The naming of the group consisted of a place name and the suffix *-mioq* (pl. *miut*) indicating "inhabitant of" the place or area in question (Rink 1875; Thalbitzer 1904; Birket-Smith 1924;)

Ethnographic descriptions of Greenland generally agree that the largest localised community, namely the winter settlement, is identical with the *miut*-group. The winter settlement comprises a number of households who in common utilise a stretch of coastal land, app. 25-30 km in length (Petersen 1965; see also Rink 1875). This association of a named group with a general territory is the accepted definition throughout the Inuit regions of *miut*-groups.[11]

Seasonal variations
The same view is expressed by Mauss in his famous study of the seasonal variations of morphology in Eskimo society. Mauss, basing his analysis of Eskimo social morphology on a comparative view of social organisation in all the Arctic, takes his basic definitions of social groupings from West Greenland[12]. To Mauss a *settlement* in its physical layout consists of:

> "a concentration of houses, a collection of tent sites, plus hunting grounds on land and sea, all of which belong to a certain number of individuals. It also includes the system of paths, passages and harbours which these individuals use and where they continually encounter one another. *All this forms a unified whole that has all the distinct characteristics of a circumscribed social group.* " (Mauss 1979: 27, emphasis added).

This definition is based on the recognition of "strictly localized", named communities of the *miut*-type, possessing "clearly recognized boundaries" and sharing basic cultural features such as language, morals and religion (pp. 27-28).

At the structural level below 'settlement' are found the *families* "united by special ties...who occupy a habitat in which they are unevenly distributed... at different times of the year" (p. 27).

At the structural level above 'settlement':

"...there are a number of social aggregates that definitely appear to have some of the features which ordinarily define a tribe. Yet, at the same time, it is apparent that more often than not these aggregates assume very uncertain and inconsistent forms; it is difficult to know where they begin and where they end. They appear to merge easily and to form multiple combinations among themselves; and rarely do they come together to perform common activities. If therefore the tribe exists, it is certainly not the solid and stable social unit upon which Eskimo groups are based. The tribe, to be more precise, does not constitute a territorial unit. Its main characteristic is the constancy of relations it permits between assembled groups. Among such groups, communications are more easily maintained than if each group seized upon its own territory and identified with it and if fixed boundaries clearly distinguished different groups from their neighbours." (Mauss 1979: 26, emphasis added)

Groups and territories

This view of the named group as coextensive with 'community' attributes to a determinate level of social organisation, the winter settlement group, all the features of 'society': a name, recognised boundaries and moral unity. This is also the place, where the objects and expressions of group unity are found (p. 58). Mauss' approach – identifying the basic structural form and the main types of ecological adaptation – is consistent with the purpose and orientation of the study, which is to examine the causes and effects of particular types of social morphology[13]. As noted in the translator's foreword, Mauss' theoretical orientation here is essentially ecological: "He examines the 'general morphology' of the Eskimo: those invariant features of the society to which a seasonal morphology can later be related" (Fox 1979: 7). These invariants are given in the relationship between Inuit and their land: "They are governed by environmental circumstances" (p. 32). The alternation between summer and winter, in combination with a certain technology, "provides the rhythm of concentration and dispersion for the morphological organization of Eskimo society" (p. 56).

This (overly structured, as also noted by the translator) perspective of Inuit society, however, hides an ambiguity with respect to the sociological reference of the analysis. Clarification is needed at several points.

What is missing in the analysis – perhaps for the reason that precise empirical information is lacking – is a recognition of the fact of *mobility*, which coexist with this apparently simple structure of dispersed, self-contained, local communities. And yet, this 'fluidity' of community may be what Mauss is aiming at in his description of group structures. If some settlements are mutually familiar and more so than with other groups, one expression may be a "certain constancy of relations" facilitating communication between the members. If these tribal-like aggregates of settlements do not have clearcut boundaries separating one from the other, how do we know that we are not talking about related groups, possibly within the same *miut*-group or 'regional band' (Correll 1976, see note 11, resp. Guemple)? Or does it indicate named groups occupying overlapping territories? Such is for instance the case in the Ammassalik district, where it has been observed that not only does the local band size greatly exceed Service's maximum level of 100 members (referred in Guemple 1972), but the name *Ammassalimmiut* exist alongside *miut*-names designating belonging to lesser local communities.[14]

There is an ambiguity in this: when are we dealing with bounded *groups* and when with bounded *territories*? Access to knowledge about territorial distribution and boundaries goes through the named groups associated with an area. But how can we be sure of the actual composition of groups? The pattern of spatial distribution of groups served to regulate hunting and protect resources (Petersen 1965). This may not have been the purpose, however (Riches 1982). The viability (once again adopting a term from ecological analysis!) of social groups within this spatial structure was dependent upon other factors than strictly ecological, or for that matter other kinds of ecological factors (ibid.). Demographic factors, for instance, influencing the composition of groups as well as the terms of their internal and external functioning, form part of what Guemple calls "population dynamics" (Guemple 1972: 106), which add to the *in*definiteness of settlement group sizes. Thus, local bands according to Guemple vary in size because of two factors: 1) seasonal variations in resource availability and 2) mobility of families between constituent local bands within, and to a certain extent between, regional bands (ibid: 84).

Fluctuations in size and composition of local communities due to periodical out-movements, emigration or immigration of households (Petersen 1965; Bobé 1937; Guemple 1972) are evidence of a relationship to land is far less permanent than what the ecological approach will have us believe. Even if the local community in Greenland seems to have been organised around a patrilineally related group (Guemple 1972: 86, referring Birket-Smith 1924), at any one time families from other settlements might temporarily or on a more permanent basis join the group habitually associated with the territory. This probably did not change their original *miut*-group affiliation, even though various mechanisms existed that "normalised" the relation of newcomers to a local community (Guemple 1972 and below).

Circles of community

The mentioned ambiguity with respect to the empirical sociological references of Mauss' work is treated in such detail here because it provides an illustrative example of a basic theoretical problem in Inuit studies: the question of the relation between *locality* and *social system*. Group form is here described as determined by technology and environment. The actual composition of the group in meaningful sociological terms is not clear and the relation between form and the process generating this form, under determinate conditions, is not clear (discussed in extenso by Riches 1982). The size of the territorial groups, the *miut*-groups "proper" (in Correll's terminology the 'deme') and their shifting distribution in space is – moving from the model to real life – further complicated by invariant factors differentiating regions from another.

The implications of this objection may be illustrated by an example: all authors agree that a fundamental organising principle of social structure is kinship. The kinship system has been defined by Guemple in these terms:

> In most of the Arctic, kinship networks can be conceived as organized into circles which feature bilateral kinship reckoning and operate on a "fade-out" principle rather than on a "cut-off" principle beyond which relatedness is not recognised." *(Guemple 1972: 85)*

This structural principle, allowing for a progressively inclusive reckoning of "relatedness" (observed also by Rink 1875), is recognised by Brody, who points out that Inuit identity in relation to land has many levels:

> There are the people of the camp, the area, the region and finally, the matter of being Inuk itself, as opposed to people of some other camp, some other area, some other region or of being *Qallunaak*/Southener, SD/ or Indian. Corresponding to such a sense of identity is a sense of belonging. Usually each nuclear family had, and may still have, a set of camps within a general area that it uses. The Kangijurlarmiut had spring, winter and summer camps (perhaps two or more for each season), that, among them, permitted the family to make year-round use of a general area. But these general areas are not demarcated, and the area of one set of camps overlaps another. Because many groups of Inuit were highly mobile, the drift from area to area, or even from region to region, brought groups who thought of themselves as quite different from one another into regular contact. Such movement even brought different groups into interdependence. Despite these exchanges, however, a sense of regional identity remained. Support for, or collaboration with, others still meant that they were, after all, *others*." (Brody 1977: 219)

The naming was not absolute but formed part of a hierarchy of names reflecting progressively widening *circles of community*, of which individuals and groups were part. As described for the Canadian Arctic, members of a village might call themselves by the name of the settlement, of the area around it or of the region, depending on whom they were contrasting themselves with or, as Brody notes with respect to an individual speaker, "on what kinds of or degree of difference he was observing between himself and others" (Brody 1977: 219). This principle is well known from all Inuit regions[15] and retained as term of reference in modern language use in all the Arctic[16]. The relativity

of the designation, however, implies that the name used is condition to historical modification, as for instance the case mentioned in Brody of the Igloolik Eskimos, *Igloolingmiut* as they are named at present, who just a few decades ago were known as *Amiturmiut* (1977: 219).

Locality and social system

Since these kin networks are ego-centred and therefore overlapping in membership, they do not form discrete elements or groups (Guemple, ibid.). This has a bearing on sociological demarcation of groups, of course. These cannot be identified in corporate terms, as they never interact as such. They can, however, be identified in terms of their residence. Since this is subject to a certain fluctuation, what is really left to study and what is of immense importance – is the concept of *-miut*, of those belonging to a place. In this term is couched important cultural notions with respect to the man-land relationship.

The theoretical premises are given by Correll, who defines the *miut*-group with reference to a number of sociological characteristics: it constitutes a dialect group, occupies a general territory, members are related by kinship, and the group constitutes a distinctive information regime (members of the group share knowledge, of places i.e., particular to the group). I will refer in some detail only two points made by Correll – one, concerning Inuit understanding of territorial boundary in strictly conceptual terms, (not talking about polity), the other concerning Inuit understanding of group:

The end of one miut-group territory and the beginning of another is decided by the use of names. Within one contiguous territory no doubling of place names are found (Riches 1982 ref. to Correll). These names are known by everybody in detail. Place names in other territories are not generally known, and if referred to are mentioned in the dialect particular for that other area, and then often with the suffix *-guuq* (equivalent to the Greenlandic *-gooq*) meaning "it is said" or "I have heard".

> "Taken together, the direct and indirect use of names relating to the environment of deme members depict an array of information which serves to identify a territory." *(Correll 1976: 176)*

> "Periphery or boundary of a territory...is that zone marked by the limits of specific knowledge, by the use of the suffix *-guuq* when referenced, by the use of terms from the appropriate neighbouring dialect and by the identification of local members who *know*." (ibid.)

The group members consider themselves related in some way to all other members of the group. A number of mechanisms were available to members who wished to extend closeness to incorporate otherwise unrelated (see Guemple's analysis of "anchillory kinship"

(1972)). Since kinship was the idiom, however determining relations according to the way it was used for practical purposes, group boundaries were "network boundaries" (Correll 1976: 176) and membership at least in principle subject to shifting alignments (ibid.).

This (miut- or 'deme') group is made up by several localised groups and in turn enter into aggregates of similar groups to form larger structures of 'tribe' (Correll) or 'cultural band' (Riches). The main point for the present purpose is the conclusion, we may draw of this discussion: it does not suffice to define the social unit, as Mauss does, in terms solely of its association with a territory, since this attributes an almost determinate relation between territory and group size and overlooks the importance of sociological factors of kinship and alignment. A *number* of informations are needed in order to define *the perception of boundaries* between groups, since these can obviously only be established by outsiders on the basis of recognition of them by the groups involved. One such important information is the system of *naming* within a territory. In terms of these considerations, boundaries are not given by ecological adaptation to a given environment of variable productivity. Boundaries are cultural constructs defined in social interaction between contiguous groups.

Greenland

The Greenlanders lived scattered along the coast in many settlements comprising a single or a few longhouses, each with a few extended families. The general pattern of residence was one of comparatively stable winter settlements alternating with summer camps of variable size, but always with the focus on the individual family. The basic social unit was the extended or joint family (Guemple 1972;) with a tendency towards an emphasis on patrilocality as the dominant principle of residence (Guemple ref. Birket-Smith 1924[17]). As previously, the form of community is described as a series of concentric circles "measured" by the entailed degree of commitment (Riches 1982) in a hierarchy of commitments leading from family via longhouse and finally settlement group (Rink 1875). It is possible to give this general empirical characterisation of Greenlandic Inuit society as it has been described since colonisation: the residence group (joined in winter settlement) is organised around the exploitation of a territory based on the individual household's alternating engagement in individual and more communal hunting activities, subordinated the ideal claim of the settlement group on a share in the catch from the common territory.

The actual composition of groups and the relation between groups at the levels mentioned from esp. Canadian material is not quite precisely established for Greenland. The settlement unit is variably composed, so it seems, of groups equivalent in composition to Guemple's local band (the exploitative band of Riches), probably equal to residents of a longhouse of perhaps 15-20 individuals. At other times a Greenlandic settlement would seem to comprise members of a number and composition equivalent to Guemple's regional band (Guemple 1972: 82ff), Riches and Correll's locational band, i.e. the *miut*-group proper).

In the pre- and early colonial period there would be an extensive mobility joining groups of families from different *miut*-territories in the large summer camps (Birket-Smith 1924; Bobé 1937; Gulløv 1986 a.o.).

Petersen (1963) relates two basic yet opposed principles of *general access to land and resources* and *privileged individual access* (rights of usufruct), which were acquired by individual families by traditional use. Usually for an individual usufruct right to become recognised, it demanded a certain investment of work to improve the quality of a place, as i.e. making a tent ring (gathering tent stones), making a stone weir, etc. These family rights lapsed if falling even momentarily into disuse, and fell back to community collective rights of use (Petersen 1963). Older writers tell of a hierarchy of rights: from collective rights – in what is washed on shore, found drifting, large animals such as whales, etc. (Dalager 1915); to communal rights of a local nature applying to the level of winter settlement. – Petersen describes, that single hunters passing through a territory risked their life, if they hunted without first approaching the settlement to ask for permission. Larger parties of visitors were not supposed to camp in a foreign territory unless first asking permission (Petersen 1963; Rink 1875; see also Riches 1982 on this point); and finally family and individual rights of usufruct (same sources).

Locality: structure or history

I believe that the preceding discussion can inform our understanding of present-day problems with respect to an integration of locality and nation in Greenland. This it can by giving us a hint of insight into the possible meanings of locality in a society and culture who relied completely on the land for its livelihood.

It seems abundantly clear from the material that in traditional Inuit society the man-land and social relationships could not be separated. If not modelled on each other – like in agrarian societies, where land is the basis for sedentary ways of living – they were grasped in terms of each other. Land was either known or unknown, named by others, in principle accessible yet subject to a certain traditional distribution[18] between exploitative groups[19] ("groups of" the land, not the other way around: the "land of" the groups (Brody 1976: 222)). Individuals and groups engaging in interaction across boundaries entered into social relations charged with meaning by reference to the principle points of orientation: groups (kinship) and territory. Of these no doubt social organisation and structure was more important than the land itself. Relations to the land form part of social relations and are realised through social relations of instruction, collaboration and sharing. Man-land relations do not constitute intrinsic relations where nothing else enters. Finally, it is in the course of engaging in social relations (being the objects of others) that individuals and groups become conscious of themselves as subjects (see also Wenzel 1986).

Considering once more the prospect of locality's contribution to the construction of identity in modern Greenland, we must try to identify the nature of the relationship between the two levels, locality and nation: as experienced by people from the inside, as far as that can be done in a general perspective – as subjects, and considered from the outside, as far as can be inferred from the representations of local communities in discourse at a national level, whereby local communities are ascribed an identity. The *imposed* identity and the *lived* identity are part of the same picture. The terms of relations between them decides which is going to win[20]. In other words: history cannot be credited with an experience of continuity between the territory and the hunters traversing it. If this continuity is there, we must see it as structurally conditioned by the part played by the hunter and his community in society at large.

Locality as centre and periphery

There is an important sense in which locality today carry a meaning reminiscent of that which it had in pre- and early colonial Greenland. Hunters and their families, whose way of life is based on the land, possess a knowledge of the environment and the named places surrounding a settlement. This way of life reflects 'community' in another and perhaps more basic sense (not to be confused with the word 'authentic', denoting 'genuine' or 'pure') than experienced in urban environments. One factor marking this difference is the commonality inherent in the fact of relying on the same source of income, in turn generating a system of mutual help as exemplified in sharing, a system of mutual information influencing individual decisions of where and when to hunt, assistance to hunters that get weather-struck, etc. Since hunting as a full-time occupation is hardly ever taken up by men, who were not brought up as hunters, a hunter is usually related to the local community by family tradition, and possess inherited rights in campsites, nettingplaces, etc.[21]

In other respects locality is a much less powerful concept than it used to be. It does not automatically make sense, and not to everybody. One expression of this is that members grow out of local communities and leave them to get an education or a job, maybe to get married. The drain of young people of marriagable

age is evident in most villages outside the regions where hunting is the economic basis. This is felt in the changing demographic composition of local settlements. Where 20 years ago villages were alive with children, these days there may be few playmates and the schools may be almost empty. If we compare with the towns during this time period, young children make up a proportionately dropping percentage of the population in the villages in general (Møller 1985). Another general trend is the change in sex ratio in the villages caused by the emigration of young women. No single explanation will do, although it is a fact that the greater emphasis on fishing, esp. (but not only) since WWII to a degree made women's work in the household redundant and in some cases almost forced emigration on them (Odgaard & Dahl 1983; Sandberg 1975).

The village community has lost its privileged position as *the* basis of individual and group orientation and has got to *make* sense out of its existence. The importance of locality is now related to 'place' and participation or 'stake' in the future. On this depends the survival in physical terms of a village, its economic foundation. – The well-being of the settlements was a major priority of the first Greenlandic Home Rule government after the election in 1979. Since then it has become increasingly obvious, however, that visions of a decentred structure of production allowing for a positive contribution of local settlements to the overall economic development have not materialised. One reason of this may be that discussions and plans of an economic nature does not consider the dimension of culture. Which, unfortunately, is not to be expected. The importance of adopting a cultural policy with respect to economic development seems evident.

Thus, there is a factor equally important to economics – for the present purpose much more interesting – which is that of cultural "viability", in the dictionary defined as 'capability of living'. This, of course, shall not be understood in any pragmatic and absolute sense but as a metaphor comprising several layers of meaning. I hope to uncover some of them, and I hope to do it in terms that can help identify relevant fields of study and open up to further empirical analysis.

Social organisation

There are in Greenland today approximately 150 inhabited places. 130 of these are settlements (villages) and 16 are towns; the remaining are isolated farmsteads of sheep-breeders in South Greenland.

Nothing would be more wrong than calling these, extremely dispersed locations 'isolated'. Habitations are local communities, bounded in space but not in their social relations. In the traditional period Greenlanders belonged to a *miut*-group and a general territory. Yet relations with other groups were established through mechanisms of alliance and kinship, making movement possible even between unrelated groups. – This principle is still valid today. Individuals belong to a *miut*-group in the sense that they come from a place, and even when they have moved away, people will often talk about this place, town or settlement, as if they belong there. They have probably retained connections with friends and relatives in this place, and it will be easy for them eventually to come back and "reconnect".

The traditional *miut*-group referred to a territory but always on the basis of group membership. The community of kindred and friends is generally less localised today than it was traditionally, when belonging to community was mediated through the social organisation of hunting or, more recently, through work at the colony. Today as before, however, social relations are channelled along lines of *alliance* and *kinship*. This means that people can move from one locality to another and, at least in general terms, quite easily find a place in the existing network[22].

The existence of an extended social network is manifest on many occasions, some of which are so general that they can for convenience be thematised:

1. The care for individuals. a) Families who hunt, whether as hunters in a small community or as part-time hunters in towns, who regularly supplement the family income from subsistence activities, usually share the meat with particular relatives, partners or neighbours. This was still practiced in Qeqertarsuaq in the Disco-Bay area, at least in the 70s and early 80s, where single women with children and elderly people could count on regular provisions of meat from brothers, brothers in law, respectively, sons and sons-in-law; *b)* Children born of young mothers are often taken care of by the mother's mother. It is a matter of course, and in some cases the child spends most of its childhood in the care of the grandparents; *c)* Grandparents, who have difficulties managing their daily round, cleaning the house or fetching water, are sometimes helped by a grandchild, a girl, who moves in with them to help.

2. Keeping relations with dispersed relatives. In Qeqertarsuaq in the 70s and 80s it was usual that at least one particular family, who had a considerable subsistence hunting (but who was otherwise not well off, having many children to bring up), regularly sent plastic tubs full of meat (containing 15-20 l) on the passenger boat to relatives as distant as Sisimiut.

3. Keeping the continuity of kindred relations in tact is supported by the tradition of passing on names of newly deceased among close relatives or close friends to the first baby born after this event.

4. Supporting relatives, subsidiary local community members etc. according to a principle of descending commitment the more distant is the relation. This applies in contexts of election to office and is an expression of

alliance. It is clearly a means of mobilising local support also in national elections, where loyalty to a local candidate is often evident in the patterns of voter support of particular candidates.

Local communities are therefore connected through the networks of their members at any one time. This gives the individual a structurally relative position vis-à-vis community and locality. Locality – acquiring importance through community membership – loses its importance to the individual if membership is relinquished. However, even if individuals leave a village or a town to live elsewhere along the coast, they often refer to their community of origin as their home community. It seems to depend on whether or not there are still relatives living in the place, i.e. on structural factors of kinship and kinship "mechanisms" applied to sustain network relations.

Local communities are all organised the same way. If the individual can attach to relatives in a community to which she is moving, she does not be*come* a member but *is* immediately part of the network. This explains how the high degree of mobility between local communities is upheld. This comprise particularly – but not only – young people and unmarried adults, who break up for a period, once in a while, to go visiting with relatives in other locations, sometimes far away. It is usually decided on very short notice, and all it takes is a ticket for the boat. Upon arrival at the destination, the visitor moves in with/attaches to a household. If the stay is extended, she may try to get a temporary job, until she eventually returns back home – or decides to establish herself in the new place.

One implication of Nuttall's analysis is that interests are highly localised. This does not seem to be valid as a general principle. The *miut*-group, before and now, is a social group, who happens to occupy a territory or locality. Attachment to this *miut*-group is mediated through relations of kinship and friendship. In the same way, the feeling for the landscape as 'community and history materialised' experienced by hunters utilising this land, is preconditioned by the part they play in the local organisation; and that, in principle, allows a man to move with his family to another place to which he is socially related and live there as a hunter. His knowledge of this area, then, has to be developed, but that happens the same way as in his home region: through participation in a community of hunters using this land. This is facilitated by the practice of *naming* territory, in which names are *partly descriptive*, following the same pattern of attributing characteristics to particular features of the landscape, and furthermore that within a region names are *not repeated*.

As in the traditional period, the local community is not important only in terms of, or even because it occupies, a place. The fact that hunters in particular must have a deep knowledge of the land they live on tend to cover up this fact. Nuttall at the same time give credit to this fact in the reference to Burghardt[23], writing that

> "His/the hunter's SD/ relationship with the environment is informed by memories, for "without memory or the sense of historic continuity the man-land relationship remains overly economic; *without economic control the relationship remains only spatial*".
> (Nuttall 1991: 15 quoting Burghardt; emphasis added)

Relations to the land form part of the system of social relations, which give access to the land, relations of co-operation and partnership, knowledge through instruction and experience, teaching the next generation. People do in fact move much more freely than in Europe without losing their "rights" to local affiliation upon return, of course within a generally agreed upon matrix of social rights and obligations. The *principle of mobility* in a sense proves that community follows channels of communication across locality, based on principles of kinship and friendship. Adherence to a group is everywhere based on the same criteria. It may be concluded therefore that "community" is established on the basis of traditional flexibility of social organisation more than on adherence to locality.

A development which has been going on in Greenland during colonialism and which is accelerating during the present years is the attachment to locality by private property, a house for instance. To a certain degree this "ownership" also applies to resources, access to which are becoming much more restricted. In traditional Greenland, before European technology was introduced, few regions ever experienced pressure on their resource base. This is different today and the problem applies to hunting as well as to fishing. Local communities feel increasingly that the interests of outsiders in local hunting events amounts to "trespassing", resulting in attempts to bolster local community control. Dahl (1990) mentions an example from Saqqaq in the district of Ilulissat (West Greenland) where fishing vessels not adhering in Saqqaq now engage in the big beluga hunt. This happens much to the discontent of the Saqqarmiut, who want to keep these very effective hunters/fishermen out of a communal event of great economic and cultural importance. However, this kind of hunt is – and was traditionally – defined as common property and therefore probably not subject to local control.

The case from Saqqaq is an example of competition for resources, which could occur also in agrarian communities in the European periphery as a result of outsiders' involvement in, for instance, buying landed resources. This would also here be resisted by local communities, who would hereby be deprived of their economic basis. This type of conflict is obviously not restricted to local scenes. On the opposite – it is symptomatic of the kind of oppositions evolving in Greenland today, which are *not between local communities* but between *interested groups on a national scale*. Concerning

the conflict between categories of primary producers this has been evident in the history of organisation of hunters and fishermen which during the 70s and 80s clearly reflected the changing structural composition of the fishing fleet and the growing differentiation or even opposition of interests between fishermen and hunters.

The influence of "interests" in determining the development of modern Greenland is felt in several respects. As noted by Dahl, 'debates in the political organs reflect conflicts at the level of local community. These evolve when resources are threatened, for instance when too many hunters or fishermen are licensed, so that resources cannot sustain the exploitation with a reasonable economic return to those hunting and fishing on a fulltime basis. This sometimes result in conflict between hunters and subsistence hunters supplementing an income based on wage earnings (Dahl 1986: 179).

Locality and nation

Local communities are related through networks of interlocking memberships integrating groups and individuals in circles of community. The relation between local community and state, however, is of a different order, that is, between structural levels.

This raises the question of *hierarchy* as an organising principle of state structures, which is lacking and in a sense in opposition to the idea of *community*, which is based on notions of egality, equal access to resources and mutual help.

If the relationship with the local environment is informed with meaning by memory (Nuttall 1991) this is an expression of the role of time and history in creating a sense of local community. It takes more than memory, however, to charge the relationship to locality with a meaning so that it can serve as a basis for orientation in the national community. It demands a knowledge of structure and your own place in it to be able to present your case to the world and construct the means to support it.

This implies a need for political representation, which is not met by many smaller communities but which has to be created anew. This often meets with a great amount of opposition, possibly for the reason that no established principles of leadership exist in settlements, that are useful for channelling community consensus (Langgaard 1986). Dahl, in the same vein describes traditional attitudes to political leaders as one of principle objection (Dahl 1984: 15). However that *"in an economic sense the traditional system of alliance is undergoing change from within the communities which is slowly erasing their egalitarian economic basis. In addition to this, there are changes brought about by the dominant political structure"* (ibid.: 16). The fact is, these years, that traditional alliances at the local level in most places seem to incorporate the new political structure of party alignment established around the period when Home Rule was in preparation. Whereas the new political structure is evidently a means of coping with changes at the national level (Dahl 1984), it is equally obvious that it is being used to forge local alliances in new terms. Oppositions and cleavages evolving in Greenland today are rooted in conflicting interests between genuine *interest organisations* of a national scale as well as *historically rooted* at a local level in principles of alliance and kinship.

It seems that modern history in Greenland has brought about roughly two kinds of local community. One that is focused, culturally and politically, another that is not focused. The term "focus" is meant to indicate a sense of common purpose or community "ethos", which is manifest in its ability to act on problems. Community ethos are probably reflections – at another level – of structural and organisational changes induced by the general movement of modernisation, which has removed the self-centredness economically and otherwise – i.e., sending the children away on school at an early age, changing cultural standards and aspirations to something that cannot be fulfilled locally, etc. etc. – causing a generation gap – a gap in the community memory.

Local communities who have been in a position where they have been able to act, to carve out so to speak, a viable economic situation for themselves (co-op production etc.), have kept up a spirit of community and a belief in their own contribution.

Local communities whose members have not been able to act in a concerted way, or who have been overtaken in time by decisions to either close the settlement down or reduce its level of economic functioning (closing the store, cut-down in loan-giving etc.) has lost this belief.

No doubt the strength of local identity influence the forcefulness of community position in matters vis-à-vis the nation. This identity, however, as I hope to have demonstrated, is not primarily local but *relational*. "*Locality*" as such, the relative difference between local communities in Greenland today, *is not the content* of cultural identity but rather a symbol of belonging developed in the interface between locality and nationality. People live in local communities, where they belong – yet a network of individual and group relations connect communities across locality. In other words: we can look for cultural differences, but they operate on the basis of a common principle.

Conclusion

The Greenlandic example shows us that locality does not in itself have a determinate influence on identity but operates as an afterthought to articulate differences in a modern national context. This is the way lo-

cality operates in the Whalsay example as well – as a boundary construction; and this is the way identity is assumed to be constructed generally – at the level of social relations.

A modern Greenlandic national identity cannot take its inspiration from *places* and peoples' attachment to *localities*, but rather to the common principle which organise people and in a sense "puts them into place" and relate them to each other. This means that a very important element is missing in Greenland today: a culture policy that can inform the construction of a development strategy (broadly conceived as comprising institutions, the social field, and economics) that in stead of separating communities on the basis of historical differences attributes to them a role in the future, based on their collective participation in a common cultural purpose. Thus, agreeing with Nuttall, that "*localitites ... illustrate the rich cultural fabric of modern Greenland*" (Nuttall 1991: 16), one purpose of this policy would be to establish the principle of continuity between past and present: not only staging cultural and political identity by putting artefacts into glass cages in museums and exhibiting them, by arranging festivals or large "folk" displays; rather, through the understanding of basic organisational principles, of how they work and on the basis of which values they operate, may a national identity become established – on top of *kalaaliussuuseq*, "being a Greenlander" which is related to *miut*-organisation: being the centre of an individual network and thus attached to several localities, yet belonging to a local community. – In this sense, the development of the Greenlandic nation may very well render new importance to an old dictum in Greenland that despite mobility of residence – you always come from a place.

Notes

1. Article partly based on a paper presented at the conference on Local Organisation, Cultural Identity and National Integration, Center for North Atlantic Studies and Centre for Cultural Research, Aarhus University, October 21-24, 1990.
2. Equivalent to the statement by several authors, notably Barth (1969) and Cohen (1982), that individuals and groups become aware of their culture when they confront its boundaries.
3. Riches (1982: 13-15) defines three historical periods of hunter-gatherer society: i) the *traditional period*, referring to "*an era prior to enduring contacts with Europeans, when a nomadic hunting and fishing economy was prosecuted, in which all necessary technology could be locally manufactured*"; ii) the *contact period* referring to "*the era subsequent to enduring contact, when a nomadic hunting, fishing and trapping economy was prosecuted, partly under the auspices of traders and missionaries, and using substantial amounts of European derived technology*"; iii) the *contemporary period*.
4. In the beginning of the printed version it says: "where he was *born*", whereas later in the same story a dialogue between father and son is recorded, in which the father says: "From the moment I *took land* at Aluk..." (Rasmussen 1924: 23, SD translation). This latter formulation is remarkably consonant with the fact that during the 17th and early 18th centuries there was an extraordinary activity of East Greenlanders ("Southlanders" or *Kujataamiut* as they were called in West Greenland) travel-

ling westward and settling here. Several factors caused a halt to this movement, which is theorized to have strongly contributed to the settlement of West Greenland (Gulløv 1986). Aluk was traditionally an important meeting place for Greenlanders from the south and east, who came here for the spring hunt of migratory seal. In the postcontact period Aluk for a time had importance as the place, where East Greenlanders acquired European goods, mainly knives. The locality lost its importance for this exchange with the establishment of the southernmost Danish colony on the west coast, after which time the South East Greenlanders themselves travelled westward (Birket-Smith 1961: 176).

5. English translation in Schultz-Lorentzen 1928: 257-259.

6. In the Danish version by Rasmussen. In the English translation he is called merely "a sealer"(Schultz-Lorentzen 1928: 257).

7. Riches (1982), basing his work on the distinction between *emic* (conceptual) and *etic* (social interactional) explanations of reasons for varying camp size, presents a theory of "dominant reasons" for joining camps in various contexts. Going through the main types of Inuit and Athapascan camps, he talks about the necessity of regional bands (equivalent to the *miut*-group mentioned later) joining together for a period of the year to rejoice "community". See also Guemple 1976: 182 suggesting the existence of a "larger community" beyond the level of the regional band.

8. In Rasmussen's editing this is a socalled *epic* legend, which may have been recorded only in this version. As such it is probably strictly localised, which is consonant with a general process of sedentarisation taking place in Greenland from the beginning of the 19th century. Gulløv informs that app. half of the tales collected in West Greenland by Rasmussen were related by South Greenlanders, possibly immigrated from the East coast (Gulløv 1986: 110).

9. I am talking here of nomadism *in principle* and not *degrees* of nomadism.

10. A most apposite remark at this point may be quoted from Riches (1982), writing about Northern nomadic hunter-gatherers: *"To be sure, we are dealing here with societies often to a great extent reconstructed by anthropologists on the basis of archival material,...Accordingly, our data on what the members of such societies knew is, at best, incomplete, and, at worst, almost completely lacking"* (p. 2).

11. Correll (1976: 172) with explicit qualifications identical with those of Brody (1976: 219), vis. that the suffix *miut*- is used relational to indicate relative belonging. There is a determinate level of *miut*-group, however, by Correll called "deme" which is the *miut*-group level associated with common territorial occupancy. This is not evident in the Greenlandic material keeping within strictly West Greenland. This presumably to do with the fact of West Greenland being first colonised, which may have changed and "fixed" settlements to a degree, which is not known until later in the other regions. See for instance Lytthans, talking about intra-regional mobility and a large number of winter settlements in the territory of Qassimiut (Lytthans 1985: 39ff).

12. Reference to Hans Egede 1741, *Det gamle Grønlands ny Perlustration*; William Thalbitzer 1904, *A Phonetical Study of the Eskimo Language,* and Henrik Rink 1875, *Tales and Traditions of the Eskimo* (as related in a note by the translator.)

13. Social morphology may be roughly defined as the physical layout of community in terms of its distribution and density of population, its land occupancy, cultural relations to objects etc.

14. The 'fluidity' of community over and above the settlement group is equally a quality of the settlement group, which – if considered over time exhibits a more or less variable composition. This is a point of empirical discussion. Damas (1969: 126, referred in Riches 1982: 15) claims a 60-70% degree of membership continuity in Central Eskimo bands. Guemple (1972: 84) invokes evidence from other groups of a high degree of interchangeability between bands over time. The question of mobility between bands no doubt cannot be taken out of the context in which it is studied. Premises of evaluating mobility such as 'duration' and 'distance' (both structural and geographical) certainly should be taken into consideration when comparing data as evidence.

15. Damas 1979: 113

16. See Birket-Smith 1924 for a reconstruction based on observations done in 1918 in the Disco Bay area. The system of naming groups, sub-groups etc. is much better known from direct observation of the various Inuit groups still leading a traditional life or with a memory of the way of life before sedentarisation. For instance see Birket-Smith (1929), concerning the Caribou Eskimos, and Brody (1977) as referred above. Dahl (1990) refers the modern use of the term in relation to *Saqqamiut's* wish to retain community control with access to local resources.

17. Albeit according to Guemple it is not supported by factual information (Guemple 1972: 105f).

18. Riches cautions us not to see this as group "ownership" or even privileged control. Lacking any formalised means of coming together apart from kinship, not needing any coordinated activity, groups outside own band were strangers and in principle enemies. The two conventional modes of approach that of "asking permission" to hunt in a foreign territory, and a traditional form of greeting – made sure that potential enmity was forgone and friendly relations could proceed (Riches 1982).

19. Petersen, explaining the existence of the principles of free resp. restricted access to land expresses it this way: on the one hand anybody could hunt freely, on the other hand "the distribution of settlements...to some degree entailed that it was not desirable just to do so" (Petersen 1963: 274ff).

20. Eidheim introduced the concept of *stigma* in the ethnicity debate: *"The traditional rejection of Lappish identity by Norwegians has deposited a stigma of inferiority in the Lappish population, which in some areas overrules all new and moral principles advocated by leaders of the movement and prevents positive response"* (Eidheim 1971: 9).

21. This does not exclude the possibility that part-time hunters, (subsistence hunting being of importance in many urban households, see Møller & Dybbroe 1978 and 1981) possess usufruct rights in particular sites, which many do. A more comprehensive system of allocation of rights is probably found in the municipalities of Thule, Upernavik, Tasiilaq and Ittoqqortoormiit, the main hunting districts in Greenland today. Outside of these regions, all districts comprise villages based on hunting and/or fishing.

22. The high degree of mobility in Greenland both between local communities in a district and between districts and regions, has not been studied in sociological terms but it is possible to illustrate implications of it. During field research in South Greenland in 1982 and '83 a statistics was made on the turnover of employees in the municipal administration. It was concluded that over a period of two years there was a numerical turnover of more than 75% of the personnel. Still considering that 25% of the employees were Danes, the shift was not caused by their premature leaving for Denmark. Counting the internal movement of personnel between departments resulted in a total figure of 100% turnover of administrative personnel within two years. – Counting movements out of the district (movements within the district are difficult to ascertain since they are not registered and have to be informed on an individual basis), counting both permanent and temporary movements of individuals (who might move back and forth several times during a year) gave a figure of a quite high percentage of "migration".

23. AA. Burghardt 1973. The bases of territorial claims. *Geographical Review 63: 244.*

References

Arima, Eugene Y. 1976. Views on land expressed in Inuit oral traditions. In: Freeman, Milton (ed.), *Inuit Land Use and Occupancy Project, II.* Ottawa: Dept. of Indian and Northern Affairs: 217-222.

Barth, Fredrik 1969. Introduction. In: Barth, F. (ed.), *Ethnic Groups and Boundaries.* Bergen, Oslo, Tromsø: Universitetsforlaget: 9-38.

Birket-Smith, Kaj 1924. Ethnography of the Egedesminde district. *Meddelelser om Grønland LXVI.* København.
1929. *The Caribou Eskimos II.* København.
1961. *Eskimoerne.* København: Rhodos.

Bobé, Louis 1936. Den grønlandske handels og kolonisations historie indtil 1870. *Meddelelser om Grønland 55(2).* København.

1937. Peder Olsen Walløes dagbøger fra hans rejser i Grønland 1739-53. *Det Grønlandske Selskabs Skrifter V.* København.

Bourdieu, Pierre 1977. *Outline of a Theory of Practice.* Cambridge: Cambridge University Press. 1986 *Distinction.* London: Routledge and Kegan Paul.

Brody, Hugh 1977. Land occupancy: Inuit perceptions. In: Freeman, Milton (ed.), *Inuit Land Use and Occupancy Project I.* Ottawa: Dept. of Indian and Northern Affairs: 185-242.

Cohen, Anthony P. 1982a. Belonging: the experience of culture. In: Cohen, A. P. (ed.), *Belonging. Identity and Social Organisation in British Rural Culture.* Manchester University Press: 1-20.
1982b. A sense of time, a sense of place: the meaning of close social association in Whalsay, Shetland. In: Op. cit.: 21-49.
1985. *The Symbolic Construction of Community.* London: Routledge.
1987. *Whalsay: Symbol, Segment and Boundary.* Manchester: Manchester University Press.

Correll, Thomas C. 1976. Language and location in traditional Inuit societies. In: Freeman, Milton (ed.), *Inuit Land Use and Occupancy Project II.* Ottawa: Dept. of Indian and Northern Affairs: 173-179.

Dahl, Jens 1984. New political structure and old non-fixed structural politics in Greenland. In: Brøsted, Jens (red.), *Native Power.* København: Akademisk Forlag.
1986. *Arktisk selvstyre.* København: Akademisk Forlag.
1990. Beluga hunting in Saqqaq. *North Atlantic Studies 2(1): 166-169.*

Damas, David 1979. The diversity of Eskimo societies. In: Lee, Richard E. & Irven deVore (eds.), *Man the Hunter.* New York: Aldine Publishing Company: 111-117.

Dybbroe, Susanne 1990a. Questions of identity and issues of self-determination. *Paper presented at the 7th Inuit Studies Conference, Fairbanks Alaska.* Ms.

Dybbroe, Susanne & Poul Brøbech Møller 1978. Fangstens betydning i dagens Grønland. *Jordens folk 13. årg. nr. 1.*

Eidheim, Harald 1971. When ethnic identity is a social stigma. In: *Aspects of the Lappish Minority Situation.* Oslo: Universitetsforlaget.

Fox, James J. 1979. Translator's foreword. In: Mauss, Marcel 1979, *Seasonal Variations of the Eskimo.* London: Routledge and Kegan Paul: 1-17.

Guemple, Lee 1972. Eskimo band organization and the "D P Camp" hypothesis. *Arctic Anthropology IX-2: 80-112.*

Gulløv, Hans Christian 1986. Straat David's grønlændere og sydlændinge. In: Petersen, Robert (ed.), *Vort sprog – vor kultur.* Nuuk: Pilersuiffik pp. 101-112.

Langgaard, Per 1986. Modernisation and traditional interpersonal relations in a small Greenlandic community: a case study from southern Greenland. *Arctic Anthropology 23 (1-2): 299-314.*

Lytthans, Kaspar 1985. *Qassimiut – nunaqarfik silasissumiittoq/ – en bygd i skærgården.* Qaqortoq.

Mauss, Marcel in collab. with Henri Beuchat 1979. *Seasonal Variations of the Eskimo. A Study in Social Morphology.* London: Routledge and Kegan Paul.

Møller, Poul Brøbech 1985. Den kulturelle og demografiske faktor i udviklingsprocessen. *Paper presented on conference by Statens samfundsvidenskabelige Forskningsråd:* "Seminar om Grønlandsforskning", Hotel Bel Air, Kastrup, June 17-18 1985, Ms.
1989. Images of Greenland in theory and political discourse. Ms.

Møller, Poul Brøbech & Susanne Dybbroe 1981a. *Om betingelserne for Grønlands kolonisering.* Dept. of Ethnography and Social Anthropology, Aarhus University. Unpublished thesis.
1981b. *Fanger/fisker – lønarbejder? En undersøgelse af sammenhængen mellem fangst og lønarbejde i Godhavn distrikt 1976 og 77.* Dept. of Ethnography and Social Anthropology. Aarhus University. Field report. Unpublished.

Nuttall, Mark 1991. Memoryscape: a sense of locality in Northwest Greenland. *North Atlantic Studies 1(2).*

Odgaard, Rie & Jens Dahl 1983. Grønlandske bygdekvinder i en økonomisk forandringsproces. *Den Ny Verden 4: 33-46.*

Paine, Robert 1974. *Second Thoughts on Barth's Models.* London: Royal Anthropological Institute Occasional Papers No. 32.

Petersen, Robert 1963. Family ownership and rights of disposition in Sukkertoppen district, West Greenland. *FOLK 5: 269-281.*
1965. Regulating factors in the hunting life of Greenlanders. *FOLK 7:107-124.*

Rasmussen, Knud 1924. *Grønlandske myter og sagn, Bd. II.* København.

Riches, David 1982. *Northern Nomadic Hunter-Gatherers. A Humanistic Approach.* London: Academic Press.

Rink, Henrik 1974 (1875) *Tales and Traditions of the Eskimo.* London: C. Hurst & Co./ København: Arnold Busck.

Sandberg, Benedikte Ingstad 1975. *Kvinnelige arbeidsmigranter ved en fabrikk i Grønland.* Oslo: Dept. of Social Anthropology. Unpublished thesis.

Schultz-Lorentzen, C. W. 1928. Intellectual culture of the Greenlanders. In: Vahl, M. et al (eds.), *Greenland II.* København: C. A. Reitzel/London: Humphrey Milford: 209-270.

Sveistrup, Poul P. & Sune Dalgaard 1945. Det danske styre af Grønland 1825-1850. *Meddelelser om Grønland 145 (1).* København.

Thalbitzer, William 1904. A phonetical study of the Eskimo language. *Meddelelser om Grønland 31.* København.

Wenzel, George 1986. Canadian Inuit in a mixed economy: thoughts on seals, snowmobiles and animal rights. *Native Studies Review 2(1): 69-82.*

Williams, Raymond 1977. *Marxism and Literature.* Oxford: Oxford University Press.

Language, Identity and Integration in the Canadian Arctic

Louis-Jacques Dorais

ABSTRACT

The manifestations of local and regional identity are numerous and involve many different social and cultural phenomena. Language is one of these phenomena. The present paper will attempt to show how Inuktitut, the language of the Canadian eastern Arctic Inuit, plays an important – albeit somewhat ambiguous – part in the assertion of their specific identity, while, at the same time, contributing to define their position within the larger Canadian society[1].

Defining identity and integration

Identity, as the word is used here, is the representation of a people's particular place in the world. It may be self-ascribed or defined by outsiders, or both. Identity is not given once and for all. The fact, for instance, of perceiving one's own reference group as being "the Inuit", "the Greenlanders", "the Canadians" or "the Danes" does not stem from a natural order of things. If I may refer to a personal example, when in my late teens, at the beginning of the 1960s, I was absolutely sure – and all my friends and relatives were sure too – that we were French Canadians. Nowadays, some twenty five or thirty years later, we are equally sure that we are not French Canadians but Québécois. In the intervening time, the evolution of the society into which we belong has led us to focus our identity on one specific part of Canada, the province of Québec, rather than on the Canadian territory as a whole.

Did our ancestry or basic culture change in between? Not at all. What actually changed – due to several factors too complex to detail here – was the way we define our relations with Canada and the rest of the world. The net result was that we progressively – and, in most cases, unconsciously – ceased to perceive ourselves as a linguistic minority, the French Canadians, in order to become a nationality, the Québécois.

Identity thus stems from the relations that one social group – or population – entertains with other groupings. Since these relations are the product of ever ongoing historical processes, identity is a dynamic phenomenon. It does not consist in a series of objective cultural characteristics, that would distinguish one population from all others. True enough, various cultural or linguistic elements may be used in order to symbolise a specific identity – it is thus allowable to speak about cultural identity – but by themselves, these elements do not constitute an identity. They are rather used as raw materials for constructing the representation that a group has of its relations with other groups and social forces. Of course, as shall be seen later on, the strength of a collective self-image can be influenced by the strength of the culture and language its bearers share, but there is no simple relation of determination between culture and identity.

As concerns integration, it is defined here as the way a group or population participates in the social system or social formation that encompasses it. Integration can vary in nature and intensity. It can be economic, political or ideological (or all of that), and may occur at different levels: local, regional, national, etc. In most – if not all – cases, it involves *unequal* relations between a dominant, integrating, group or society and a dominated, integrated, one.

The integration of the Inuit within Canadian society

Contemporary Inuit history may be analysed as a process of progressive integration within Canadian society. At the beginning of the Second World War the Inuit had been participating since many decades in the capitalist mode of production as petty commodity producers and they had already adopted Christianity. They entertained relations of economic dependence towards the commercial interests represented by the Hudson Bay and other trading companies. These companies established the rules of trade – for their own benefit of course – and fixed prices unilaterally. They maintained many Inuit producers in debts and controlled their access to supplies such as flour, sugar, tea, firearms, ammunition and steel traps, which had become essential to the natives.

But on the other hand, at the beginning of the 1940s, the traditional social relations, based on cooperation and sharing, were still dominant in the hunting camps. The majority of the Inuit population was nomadic, visiting the trading post and the Christian mission once or twice a year. The situation in the Canadian Arctic thus corresponded to what some scholars define as internal colonialism: southern economic and political interests, foreign to the local population, had imposed to this population a *commercial, juridical* through the presence of the Royal Canadian Mounted Police, and *ideological* (religious) system upon which local people had no control, even if in everyday life, the major part of their existence was still organised according to traditional social relations, and had nothing to do with national institutions.

Things began to change in the late forties, when the Canadian federal government decided to establish in the North an extensive network of public schools, health stations and administrative centres which were to cater to the needs of the Inuit. This decision was motivated by various factors – such as the newly discovered economic and strategic importance of the Arctic – which made it imperative, in the eyes of the Canadian establishment, to put the North in tune with the rest of the country.

In order to achieve this, the northern citizens were to gain access to the same services as those offered to the general population. This would transform them, according to an expression often heard among bureaucrats during the late fifties, into "average Canadians". The public policy for the North was thus one of normalisation. Thence the enormous development, sponsored by the State, that was to be observed from 1948 to 1965: establishment of some 50 public elementary schools all over the Inuit territory; construction of several secondary boarding schools, one for each region; opening of nursing stations, supported by four regional hospitals; establishment of an elaborate administrative structure, with resident Northern Service Officers and agents for economic development; creation of cooperatives, in order to develop commercial fisheries, carving and other handicrafts.

The Inuit thus became full-fledged participants in the Canadian institutions, although their social status remained one of dependent and marginal populations, without anything to say about their own development, since all decisions were taken by non-Inuit civil servants and politicians.

The results of this policy were not long to be felt: complete sedentarisation of all Inuit bands (in 1965, 95% of all arctic natives lived in some 50 permanent villages); schooling in English for the young people, with a generalisation of bilingualism; improvement of health and sanitary conditions; development of wage work; etc. The impact of these changes was particularly strong among the young people, schooled in a language and along a cultural model completely unknown to their parents. But despite this confusion, the Inuit did not lose their identity. Their geographic isolation, the fact that a very few foreigners had settled amongst them, and the vitality of their cultural representations contributed to preserve their notion of belonging to a territory and a way of life completely different from those of the other Canadians. Among the young people, this sense of identity, allied with the acquisition, thanks to the schools, of some knowledge about the outside world, entailed the emergence, at the beginning of the 1970s, of a generation able to claim the economic, political and cultural rights that nobody had yet recognised them.

Because of the conjuncture, the struggle for these rights was then felt as an urgent necessity by the Inuit. Factors such as major projects in the field of economic development – the Mackenzie Valley pipeline and the James Bay hydroelectrical project for instance – encouraged the arctic natives to form aboriginal associations: *Committee for Original Peoples Entitlement* (1970); *Inuit Tapirisat of Canada* (1971); *Northern Québec Inuit Association* (1971); *Labrador Inuit Association* (1973). These associations succeeded in organising the claims of the Inuit and in defending the interests of their members. In 1975, the Northern Québec Inuit Association signed the James Bay Agreement. In 1976, Inuit Tapirisat of Canada presented a proposal for dividing the Northwest Territories into two parts, in order to create a new province (Nunavut) with an Inuit majority. An agreement-in-principle on this question was reached almost thirteen years later, in the spring of 1990.

Such events entailed major modifications in the northern administration. In Arctic Québec for instance, following the James Bay Agreement, native bureaucratic structures were established: a regional administration, *Kativik Regional Government*; twelve municipalities; an economic corporation, *Makivik Corporation;* a school administration, *Kativik School Board*, with special powers in the fields of curriculum development and teacher training; a consultative body dealing with health services, *Kativik Regional Council on Health and Social Services*; etc.

Nowadays then, the situation is very different from what it was twenty years ago. Everywhere in Canada, Inuktitut is now taught in the schools, up to grades II or III, and the Inuit are abundantly consulted about almost everything. They also possess some administrative authority. But the real political power – and the juridical framework within which the native institutions must function – still lie in the hands of the southern Canadian politicians and bureaucrats, and of their economic supporters.

In this way, the Inuit now belong to the techno-bureaucratic system. In many instances, they possess their own administrative institutions, staffed with native personnel, but these are modelled upon their southern Canadian equivalents, to which they are intimately linked, and from which they often receive their orders. The economic regime is one of State capitalism, since most of the available capital is alloted by the federal or Québec provincial government and is administered by native public corporations. Private entrepreneurship is somewhat encouraged, but it functions on a very small scale, and here again, the only readily available capital comes from the State.

The integration of the Inuit into the Canadian society is thus complete. They are no longer a marginal population, but an integral – albeit economically and politically dependent – part of Canada. This is why most Canadians do not consider them any more like an exotic and somewhat foreign people, as was the case up to twenty years ago, but as an ethnic minority which has its place, along with other such minorities, in a multicultural Canada, or, at best, as a dependent nation – the official discourse currently uses the expression "first nations" – entitled to preserve its language and customs within the political jurisdiction of Canada and the provinces.

The Inuit, however, do not view themselves in the same way. They feel that they constitute a full-fledged aboriginal nation and/or a distinct regional arctic society which should be master of its own destiny. Their identity is, thus, in conflict with the perception that many other Canadians – seemingly including the federal and provincial States – have of them. This perceptual conflict, which stems from the different structural positions of natives and non-natives within Canadian society, may entail severe consequences. As an ethnic minority, the Inuit are entitled to cultural and linguistic rights and to some administrative autonomy. But as a distinct nation or society, they also may claim economic and political self-rule. There is a big enough difference.

Language and identity

In this context, the language of the Inuit, *Inuktitut*, has become a sort of indicator of Inuit identity, although its meaning and value are at variance when one looks at them from the national or local points of view.

At the national level, the position of Inuktitut may be considered as that of an ideological object, i.e. of a symbolic stake representing the rights of the Inuit, as they are perceived by the State and its economic supporters on the one hand, and by the native organisations and corporations, on the other.

For the federal and provincial governments and bureaucracies, and for most of the Canadian majority society, language and culture are at the heart of the debate over native rights. They feel that each Inuk (or,

for that matter, Amerindian) individual has the personal right to maintain his or her ethnic identity, by being allowed to preserve and transmit his native language and culture. In a way then, the limited administrative powers and land titles that may be granted the Inuit are merely considered as means to implement this goal of protecting individual rights. A good example of this point of view is found in the report of the *Special Joint Committee of Parliament on Canada's International Relations* (Simard & Hockin 1986). One of the conclusions reached by this report is that Canada should work at strengthening "Inuit cultural autonomy", and that the means best suited to attain this goal include the development of new northern political institutions and the settlement of land claims.

This explains why the government is willing to encourage, both morally and financially, the teaching of Inuktitut, its visibility in the media – where Inuktitut is heard all over the North on radio and, more occasionally, on television – and its use as a semi-official language. For instance, an effort is made for providing some public services in the native tongue. As part of this effort, literally hundreds, if not thousands, of pages of administrative and technical texts are translated annually into Inuktitut. Most of them are completely useless. Those people who read English largely prefer this language to their native dialects, as far as written matters are concerned. And those who do not would have problems understanding the jumble of neologisms and borrowed words found in these texts. But the government and private corporations, who spend important sums on these translations, feel that they have done their duty for the preservation of Inuit identity.

Language is also considered important by the native organisations. For them, however, its preservation does not constitute a goal by itself. Its importance rather lies in the fact that it symbolises the collective rights of the Inuit, whether they be territorial, economic, political or cultural. The use and transmission of Inuktitut are publicly encouraged, as such encouragement is useful to the management of native identity, but when it comes to assessing the relative weight of language and culture among the priorities of most Inuit associations and corporations, they very often come in last position, after economic development and political autonomy – with the consequence that most linguistic and cultural projects undertaken by the native organisations do not last for long and do not produce much in terms of social and educational results.

At the national level then, Inuktitut is more a symbol than a reality. The recognition by the State of the linguistic rights of the Inuit has nevertheless had some positive consequences. The native language is now taught in the schools and heard on the electronic media. But this recognition can be precarious. In its budget for 1990, the federal government, eager to decrease the national deficit, did not hesitate to cut down most of the funding allotted to the Inuit Broadcasting Corporation and to a majority of the native periodicals. What is more important is that the government is constantly trying to transfer the Inuit's struggle for economic and political autonomy to a less menacing arena, that of cultural and linguistic questions.

The contrasting but somewhat analogous positions on language held by both Inuit and non-Inuit national institutions reflect their respective definitions of native identity. Such clearcut positions are not found at the local level, that of the arctic communities. Village people participate in, and are affected by, the national organisations, but their centres of interest differ from those of the politicians, whether native or non-native. In the Inuit communities, language and culture are not mere ideological objects. They are facts of daily life. The speakers of Inuktitut partake in a semantic universe which stands very far from our own. Michèle Therrien, an ethnolinguist from Paris' INALCO, *Institut National des Langues et Civilisations Orientales*, has shown that the Inuit lexicon for the human body (cf. Therrien 1987), health and illness, moral concepts, etc., reflects semantic categories and a structure of meaning that have nothing to do with the concepts we are familiar with. In Inuktitut for instance, there are no words for guilt, culpability, sentence or penalty. No wonder then that the arctic natives constantly complain about the inadequacy of the judicial and social services they receive, insisting on the fact that the non-Inuit – and acculturated Inuit – agents operating these services are unable to understand their real needs.

There is no doubt that in the localities where the native language and culture are still strong, they contribute to consolidate the identity of their users. Inuit speakers and culture bearers do not have much problems finding, in their daily life, enough material for constructing a relatively positive image of their position in the contemporary world. For them, far from principally being ideological symbols whose manipulation has a political effect, language and culture represent the basis of their identity.

Objectively speaking however, and despite the fact that in the Canadian eastern Arctic with the exception of Labrador, Inuktitut is spoken by over 85% of the aboriginal population, the native tongue now survives in a context of diglossia. This means that even at the local level, the Inuit as a whole need two languages, if they want to function properly within the Canadian social formation. Inuktitut is not enough to cope with the complexities of modern life. English – and French, in Arctic Québec – is also necessary.

The two (or three) languages in presence do not hold an equal status. One of them, the vernacular, is mainly used for private conversations, local transactions and lower level education, as well as for a few more prestigious, but highly symbolical functions – cf. its use as an official language in the Legislative Assembly of the Northwest Territories. The other language, English, is used for administration (except at a very local level), higher (i.e. beyond grades II or III) education, skilled work, and on television. Despite the real prestige of Inuktitut, English is generally considered by the Inuit as much more useful if one wants to make his or her way in life.

In their study of language attitudes in an Arctic Québec trilingual community – where 75% of the 1,100 residents have Inuktitut as their first language, 15% French and 10% English – Taylor and Wright (1989) show that if Inuktitut still remains "strong and vibrant" among the Inuit, the lingua franca of the community is clearly English:

> "Despite the fact that Anglophones make up less than 10% of the population, English is the preferred second language of both the Inuit and Francophones. Moreover, English is viewed as very important to life in the community by all three language groups. Of primary interest is the dominance of English in the work context and the resulting elevation of prestige attained because of this." (Taylor & Wright 1989: 105)

Thus, the inherent strength of Inuktitut, still spoken and used by the almost complete Inuit population, can be jeopardised by the fact that English is becoming increasingly dominant in the economic field, and among young people in general (Taylor & Wright 1989: 115).

This means that the linguistic and cultural bases upon which local identities are built may be suffering severe erosion. This would be a natural outcome for a diglossic situation, where the linguistic phenomena reflect and reinforce the dominant social relations. After all, it is normal that the economic and political dependence of the Inuit entail a linguistic dependence upon English, and this, in spite of the high symbolic value of Inuktitut.

Identity at the community level: the case of Puijilik

In order to better understand how language and identity are interlocked at the local level, I will now briefly describe the sociolinguistic situation in a small Arctic Québec community. My data are preliminary. They are drawn from 18 in-depth interviews conducted in Inuktitut, in June 1990, among members of this community. The sample includes eight male and ten female respondents, ages ranging from 15 to 67 years old with an average of 43.5 years of age.

Puijilik (this is a pseudonym) lies towards the eastern end of Hudson Strait. At research time, it harboured a population of 211 persons, 198 of whom were Inuit and 13 non-Inuit. These last included eight francophone Québécois, three English Canadians, one anglophone Mohawk Indian and one Turkish immigrant who spoke some English. None of them fully understood Inuktitut.

In Puijilik, primary hunting and fishing activities are still important, but not on a commercial basis since the EEC ban on the import of seal skins. All of the men regularly hunt caribou, sea mammals and migratory birds. Most people also fish for trout and arctic char. Fox trapping, however, has almost completely disappeared.

The produce from these activities is exclusively for local consumption. Money comes from wage work and government subsidies. The 111 persons over 15 years old who are permanent residents of the village (this excludes seven of the non-Inuit) share some 40 different jobs. Except for two small private enterprises – a variety store and a distributor of petroleum products – all jobs are linked to the provincial, regional and municipal administrations, the school, the nursing station, and the cooperative.

The village is run by a municipal council. At the time of my visit, the mayor, a woman, was also principal of the local school and had just finished a mandate as president of the cooperative. Apart from the municipal council, the following committees are found: education committee, health committee, housing committee, landholding committee, alcohol and drug committee, board of directors of the cooperative, Anglican church council, Anglican women's council, Pentecostal church council. Most of these local committees send delegates to their regional counterparts. The Puijilik people thus participate very actively in the administrative structures put in place by the James Bay Agreement.

Inuktitut is the main language of the community. It is the almost exclusive means of communication in all Inuit homes, on the street, at church, on the local radio, as well as during hunting and fishing expeditions. The native language is also commonly heard in the work place, except for the linguistic interchanges with non-Inuit co-workers. In this case, English is used except at the nursing station, where the interpreter is a French speaking Inuk, whatever the mother tongue (French, English or Turkish) of the interlocutor. In fact, the only place where Inuktitut *is not* heard that much is the school, which employs five non-Inuit teachers, and where beyond grade II, all students are required to speak the language in which they are taught, English or French.

As a rule, all Puijilik Inuit under 45 years of age can speak some English and, among several younger ones, some French also. Despite this fact, however, everybody speaks Inuktitut in the family, although some parents may occasionally use English words and expressions when speaking to their children. Conversely, some children try, from time to time, to address their parents and grandparents in English, but they are normally answered in Inuktitut. In the mixed families – there are six couples where the husband is not an Inuk – the children speak Inuktitut with their mother and among themselves, but use French or English when addressing their father.

People belonging to the generation aged 25 to 40 years old, schooled exclusively in English, tend to mix this language with Inuktitut when speaking to their peers. This is not the case for the older generation, who had practically no schooling, nor for the younger one, who frequented schools where some Inuktitut was taught.

All Puijilik Inuit, whether schooled or not, are able, with various skills, to read and write Inuktitut in syllabic characters. Those who are bilingual, but have not received much schooling, can also read English, but Inuktitut is easier for them. For those with a little more formal schooling – typically, those who have completed elementary school – Inuktitut is easier to write, but they read better in English. Finally, those Inuit who have completed or gone beyond high school find it easier to read and write English (if they have only been taught in this language), or do not have problems in any language, if they have had some Inuktitut at school.

All this shows that Inuktitut is still very important in Puijilik. One may wonder, however, if it really is the dominant language. As we have just seen, many bilinguals, including several teachers of Inuktitut, are more at ease with English when it comes to reading and writing. Moreover, English is the *lingua franca* of the community, as Inuktitut is not spoken by the non-Inuit residents. When it comes to communications beyond the village limits, almost everything, including interaction within the Inuit organisations, is done in English. English is also the language most commonly heard on television and video cassettes – two cassette outlets are found in the village. Like the community studied by Taylor and Wright, then, Puijilik is witnessing a situation of diglossia. Inuktitut is not sufficient by itself to permit local people to function adequately within Canadian society. They must also resort to English and, to a much lesser extent, French.

The Puijilik Inuit are conscious of this situation. All of them agree on the importance of knowing English and/or French. For two-thirds of my sample (12/18), these languages are necessary if one wants to work adequately or, in other words, to make one's own way in life. Four other respondents stress the fact that northern society has now become bilingual or even trilingual. Most informants, however, insist that the first language of the Inuit should still be Inuktitut, and that English and French should be learned as second or third languages only.

In fact, all of our respondents consider the knowledge and use of Inuktitut as indispensable to the Inuit. For twelve of them, the native language is linked to their basic identity. Typical statements include the following: "The Inuit are characterised by their language" – "If we lose our language, we will be like White people" – "My thoughts and my heart can only be expressed through Inuit words". Several other informants insist on the fact that the Inuit need Inuktitut because they feel more comfortable when speaking this language.

Such assertions about the respective importance of the native and non-native languages reflect underlying assumptions on the interface between traditional culture and contemporary life. For the Puijilik Inuit, the activity most essential to the preservation of native identity is *maqainniq*, or "going on the land" – for hunting, fishing or trapping. The majority of our respondents assert that without *maqainniq,* the Inuit would not be Inuit any more. *Maqainniq* is taught to children and young people within the extended family and is conducted in Inuktitut. Most informants consider it the occasion par excellence for learning and practicing the native language.

Nowadays, however, *maqainniq* does not permit economic survival. One must, thus, also learn about *kiinaujaliurutiit*, "means for making money", i.e. abilities for wage work. These do not stem from Inuit culture. They are rather introduced, taught and controlled by White people. This is why the best place to learn them is at school, whose prime function seems to be the transmission of some useful *kiinaujaliurutiit.*

Since *kiinaujaliurutiit* are basically White people affairs, the White people's languages, English and French, are two of the most useful "means for making money". It is thus considered as normal if the main school languages are those of the non-Inuit.

Inuktitut is nevertheless taught in the Puijilik school. Kindergarten, Grade I and Grade II are entirely in this language. Beyond Grade II, however, the native tongue is only used for teaching Inuit culture and some vocabulary. For all other subjects, English or French (at parents' choice) are the only teaching media. The parents generally put some of their children in the English classes and some others in the French ones.

As Inuktitut still remains the preferred language of the population, everybody approves of the fact that it is taught in the school. But respondents are divided about the real usefulness of the teaching offered. Half of the sample find that school really helps kids knowing their language better, but the other nine informants state that it offers little or no help in this domain. Some of these last think that school would be really helpful if Inuktitut served as a teaching medium for subjects such as grammar, mathematics, biology and social sciences, and this up to Grade VIII, the uppermost available grade in Puijilik.

The linguistic bases upon which part of the local Inuit identity is built thus seem solid, although challenged by the unavoidable presence of English and French, the languages of *kiinaujaliurutiit*. In the minds of most Puijilik Inuit, there exists a strong link between native language and identity. Indeed, two thirds (12/18) of the sample think that one cannot be labelled an *inutuinnaq* (a "real Inuk") if one does not speak Inuktitut. Those six respondents who do think that a "real Inuk" may not speak Inuktitut assert that language is important, but that if one has Inuit parents, he or she will always remain an Inuk, even without a knowledge of the language.

When asked how do they define themselves, twelve of our informants (not necessarily the same as in the above paragraph) state that they are *inutuinnait*, "real Inuit". The other six rather prefer to call themselves *nunalituqait*, "old time possessors of the land", a recently coined word for aboriginal people. Among these last are found four of the five women born before 1937 included in our sample.

The Puijilik Inuit realise that the basis of their identity may be in jeopardy. When asked if their grandchildren and great-grandchildren will preserve Inuit language and culture, ten of our informants answer a clear "no". Six others utter a cautious "yes": the native tongue and customs can only be preserved if the individuals, the community and the school make a special effort to save them. Only two respondents think that linguistic and cultural survival presents no problem.

We may conclude, then, that in Puijilik, the status of Inuktitut is fragile, even if this language is in everyday use in the community. As a consequence of the integration of the local people in the national institutions, English and, in a lesser way, French, are becoming increasingly dominant. The fact that most institutions are now run by Inuit does not seem to change much with respect to this diglossic situation. The school, for instance, is primarily perceived as a place where one learns English, French and other "means for making money" *(kiinaujaliurutiit),* since the traditional land activities *(maqainniq)* are not sufficient any more for making a living. This may mean that in the long run, the identity of the Puijilik Inuit will lose its present basis.

Conclusion

This paper has shown how language plays a differential but important role in defining the identity of the Canadian Inuit and in contributing to integrate them into the national society. At the local level, most natives of the Arctic consider their language as the best means for expressing their "thoughts and heart", to quote one of my informants, and to help supporting their most basic identity. But they also acknowledge that English (and French in Québec) is necessary if one wants to participate in the labour market and social organisation of the contemporary Canadian Arctic.

At the national level, the Inuit and non-Inuit organisations tend to treat Inuktitut as an ideological object. The Inuit politicians stress its importance, but this importance stems from the fact that it stands as a symbol of aboriginal economic and political collective rights, rather than from its intrinsic value. As for the State and its backers, they consider Inuktitut as belonging to the kind of individual linguistic and cultural rights that are normally granted to anybody belonging to an ethnic minority. This whole situation is a consequence of the progressive integration of the Inuit within the Canadian social formation.

The role of Inuktitut, then, can be summarised as follows:

Local communities:
Preferred means of expression and language of traditional activities

Definition of identity

National native organisations:
symbol of collective rights

National integration

State and non-native bureaucracies:
means for fulfilling obligations towards members of an ethnic minority

It thus appears that the contemporary integration of the Inuit within Canadian society has led to contrasting, if not contradictory, definitions of the role and value of their language and culture. How will the local people cope with this situation? Are they doomed to progressively lose the linguistic and cultural bases of their self-definition? Not necessarily. Their strong attachment to their language, territory and way of life

and, also, the existence of local organisations such as the cooperatives and churches, very weakly linked to the native and non-native bureaucratic structures, may help them to preserve their most basic identity.

Notes

1. Revised version presented at the international symposium on Local Organisation, Cultural Identity and National Integration in the North Atlantic and the Arctic, Aarhus University, Denmark, October 22-24, 1990. Apart from my own field work (funded by the Social Science and Humanities Research Council of Canada), data for this paper have been drawn from Prattis & Chartrand 1984, Stairs 1985 and Taylor & Wright 1989. Some of the ideas found here have already been expressed in Dorais 1988a, 1988b, 1988c, 1989 and 1990.

References

Dorais, L.J. 1988a. "Inuit Identity in Canada". *Folk* 30: 23-31.
1988b. "Sois belle et tais-toi: la langue des Inuit dans le Canada actuel". *Études/Inuit/Studies* 12(1/2): 235-243.
1988c. "Langue, identité et philosophie du développement nordique." In: G. Duhaime (ed.) *Le développement des peuples du Nord*. Actes du premier colloque Québec-Russie, Québec: Université Laval, Groupe d'études inuit et circumpolaires: 21-28.
1989. "Bilingualism and diglossia in the Canadian Eastern Arctic". *Arctic* 42(3): 199-207.
1990. "The Canadian Inuit and their language.": In: (D.R.F. Collis, ed.) Arctic Languages. An Awakening (D.R.F. Collis, ed.), Paris: Unesco: 185-289.

Prattis, I. & J.P. Chartrand 1984. *Minority Language Bilingualism: The Case of Inuktitut in the Canadian North*. Ottawa: Carleton University, Department of Sociology and Anthropology (Departmental Working Paper 84-3).

Simard, J.M. & T. Hockin 1986. *Independence and Internationalism: Report of the Special Joint Committee on Canada's International Relations*. Ottawa: Queen's Printer.

Stairs, A. 1985. "The development context of native language literacy: Inuit children and Inuktitut education". In: (B. Burnaby, (ed.), *Promoting Native Writing Systems in Canada*, Toronto: OISE Press.

Taylor, D.M. & S.C. Wright 1989. "Language Attitudes in a Multilingual Northern Community". *The Canadian Journal of Native Studies* 9(1): 85-119.

Therrien, M. 1987. *Le corps inuit*. Paris: SELAF/Presses universitaires de Bordeaux.

Ethnic Integration and Identity Management

Discourses of Sami self-awareness

Vigdis Stordahl

ABSTRACT

The article focuses on the accelerating process of change which the Sami society has undergone during the last 20-30 years. It is described how this process has had twofold character. On the one hand, there is a strategy of planned integration of the Sami community into the nation state. On the other hand and at the same time a process of ethnic incorporation is going on which leads to an integration into a Sami nation. This process has created the basis for a revitalization of Sami culture and for the development of an intraethnic discourse about how to be a Sami in the modern world, Samiland has inevitably become a part of.

During the last 20-30 years Sami society has been characterized by an accelerating process of change. This process has had a twofold character. On the one hand, their has been a planned process of integration of the Sami community into the nation state. On the other hand, at the same time, a process of ethnic incorporation has been going on which leads to an integration into a Sami nation. These two processes are running parallel, the one presupposing the other.

In this article I would like to show how the new opportunity situation has created the basis for a revitalization of Sami culture and the development of an internal (intraethnic) discourse about how to be a Sami in the modern world Samiland has inevitably become part of.

After World War II there has been a marked change in Norway's minority policy. The German occupation of Norway, especially the burning down of the two northernmost regions (North-Troms and Finnmark) and the concomitant evacuation of the population, caused the emergence of a sense of solidarity on the part of Norwegians for the population in the North, including the Sami. This effected a change in the opportunity sitation of the Sami. The political climate was no longer favourable for a policy that was founded on an idea of the superiority of one of the groups, namely the Norwegians. The commitment which Norway put into the United Nation's work at The Declaration of Human Rights was another nail in the coffin of the old Socio-Darwinistic ideas. A democratic and humane nation which had committed herself to the idea of equal rights in the Declaration of Human Rights, could not risk being suspected not to fullfil these ideas within her own borders (Eidheim 1971).

Yet, still some years were to come before these new ideas became politically binding vis-à-vis the Sami. The areas burned down by the Germans had first to be rebuilt. The Norwegian government decided, however, that the regions not only should be rebuilt but were to be raised to the social and economic standards of the South. The North should no longer be just a strategic – albeit important – outpost, but was to become a part of the Nation. Norwegians from the South were asked to show solidarity and go north to help rebuild the country. In retrospect we have to admit that it was an impressive work that was done to raise the North. In 20-30 years' time the region has been turned from a ruin to modern villages and towns. The Welfare State has reached the smallest out-of-the-way-place.

There is, however, always a reverse side of the medal. What soon became evident, was that the Sami lacked skills to be able to take advantage of what was offered by the welfare-state. To many Sami the question became one of *either* ethnic identity *or* an acceptable standard of living (Minde 1980:102). As one Sami, working as a sheriff's assistant during the early post-war years, put it:

> "Most of my time was spent helping people who had no skills in filling formulas and writing letters. I then realized more than ever how important it was for a Sami to learn Norwegian – yes, in fact becoming a Norwegian."
> (Nordlys 22.11.80, cited from Minde op.cit.:102)

A more principal stand, a clearer goal and instructions for the work with Sami-related questions, was asked for, and in 1956 the government appointed a Commission to look into these questions. The commission's task was to:

"... Consider the principal questions of the Sami situation in society and propose specific economic and cultural action that can help the Sami achieve competence so they can take fully part in society." (Samekomiteen p. 5)

The commission, which is best known as the Sami Commission, released its report in 1959. The report stressed the importance of mutual respect between the two groups, Sami and Norwegians. It also stressed the importance of giving the Sami the opportunity to develop a pan-Sami sense of solidarity. A succesful re-establishment of a sense of cultural security among the Sami, as well as mutual respect between the two communities, demanded however that equal social and economic opportunities be guaranteed. Following Norwegian practice, the commission report was circulated to appropriate bodies. On the basis of their comments, the Department of Education issued a report to *Stortinget*, the Norwegian parliament. In May 1963, Parliament discussed the report, and all the MPs agreed that previous minority policy now belonged to the past. The Sami were to become equal members of the Nation. But, and this is important, this equality was to be enjoyed by Sami in their *individual* capacity and not as members of a separate ethnic *group*. This was expressed in the distinction between "Sami-speaking Norwegians and Norwegian-speaking Norwegians". While the Sami Commission talked about mutual respect and recognition between *ethnic groups*, the department and Parliament talked about the respect between *individuals*. This had, of course, consequences for initiatives taken to realize this equality. The main contribution from the State was to be general welfare-political means such as schools, health and social services, social housing programmes, and economic development. Special attention had to be paid to the language situation, for instance by removing a discriminatory clause in the Land Sales Act of 1902, – a clause that prevented any sale of land to a person who could not prove his skills in Norwegian – furthermore, by introducing the right to choose the Sami language in school and making sure that Sami names on the maps were spelled correctly.

The basic view in dealing with the "Sami question" now became that the Sami had *general problems* which were of the same order as those of marginal regions as such in Norway, and *special problems* which had to do with language and cultural background. If we take a look at the means introduced, we soon see that the distinction between the special means and the general ones are not that obvious. Often the special means has had the character of reinforced general means or delayed ones to keep track with the development in the rest of the country (Aarseth 1978: 243).

The new interest for and focus on the "Sami problem" was not only a result of the Sami Commission's report and Parliament's assent. Important participants in this movement were the Sami themselves. They took advantage of the new opportunity situation created after World War II and started organising, nationally as well as on a Nordic level. A Sami Association was established in Oslo in 1947 and reorganized in 1951 to a nationwide association. Parallel to this national organisation, a Nordic Sami Council was established in 1956. But not until the Sami in the interior of Finnmark – the so-called Sami core area because in this region the Sami are the majority – started to organise themselves locally, did things go ahead. During the 60s Sami associations were started in all the municipalities here. By 1968 the time had come to reorganise the nationwide organisation from 1951, and *Norgga Samiid Riikasearvi* /The Norwegian Association of Sami, was a reality. During the 70s a lot of local associations joined. These were associations outside the core-area, from the southern territories (in Norwegian: *Fylke*) and from the bigger cities. In 1975 the Sami went international by joining the World Council of Indigenous Peoples (WCIP). During the 60s and 70s we are witnessing an ethnic incorporation never seen before in Sami history, and the ethnopolitical organisations become a factor in Norwegian as well as Nordic politics. We all remember the struggle over the Alta-Kautokeino hydro-electrical power plant scheme.

This focusing on the North in general and on the situation of the Sami especially, canalized public money to the Sami regions, money which, among other things, was used in building Sami institutions like a Sami radio, a Sami high-school, a Sami museum, a Sami newspaper, a Sami research institute, a Sami teachers' training college, just to mention a few. The ideas behind and request for such insitutions came from local Sami politicians and the newly established ethnopolitical organisations. The national government supported the ideas, partly because they felt obliged to support Sami culture, partly because these new institutions meant new job opportunities in a region that lacked it desperately. Some of these institutions became separate posts in the national budget (the Sami museum), while others became affiliated with nationwide institutions (the Sami radio). And most important, the positions as journalists, researchers, technicians, curators and teachers were mostly filled by qualified Sami, and not by southerners as is the case in the north of Canada, Alaska and in Greenland. The reason for this is twofold. Firstly, education was looked upon as the main tool for integrating the North into the nation state, and was therefore given priority and a lot of resources. The new educational model of nine years of compulsory schooling, it was decided, was to be implemented first in two Sami municipalities. Secondly, the Sami youths quickly understood the possibilities inherent in this new model to qualify themselves for further education. Besides, their parents supported and encouraged them, even though they knew that education meant leaving home and Sami culture.

Education was a qualification for participating in Norwegian society. In the mid-60s, when the new school model was introduced, few of the youths or their parents saw any possibilities to use an education in the Sami villages. At the universitites and colleges in the South, however, not only did young Sami learn a profession, they also came in contact with new ideas about what it meant to be a Sami in the modern world, ideas introduced by the newly established Sami movement. "We learned to become Sami politicians", as one expressed it to me.

The small-holder's daughter and son have become a teacher and a nurse, a fact which we can read out of official statistics. In the small Sami town where I have been doing research lately, 70% was in 1950 occupied in primary activity like farming and reindeer herding. Twenty years later, in 1970, the proportionate number was 40.5% and in 1980 only 17.5%. The proportionate increase has come in business and service occupations, so that today almost 70% are occupied in these sectors. What statistics also tell us is that this change in occupation was at its peak during the 70s. Between 1970 and 1980 the town got 119 new jobs in health and social services and 88 in education. This change is also reflected in the pattern of settlement. Today 93% of the 2700 inhabitants live in the town centre, which during these years has developed from a small village consisting of a few farmers, a sheriff, a priest and a doctor, to a modern town – to the "capital of Sami-land" as some like to put it.

Not all who have analysed these processes will agree that we are also witnessing an integration into a Sami nation. One of those who have strongest opposed this view is Tim Ingold (1976). In his book *The Skolt Lapps Today* he strongly opposes and criticizes the whole foundation of the Sami movement.

"... Far from having any objective existence in contraposition to a majority, the source of the 'minority culture' lies in the minds of a rather small elite who can establish some connection with the Lappish milieu but whose values, couched in terms of extreme generality, are of wholly external derivation." (p.245)

"It is of course for the ideologies of the Lappish movement themselves, many of whom are successful practioners in education, law, commerce and administration, that the establishment of such a claim is most important." (p.238)

Ingold is right that it was a small group who started it all, and that most of them were well educated. It is also easy to point to contradictions in the ideological foundation of the movement, as Ingold does. But if we take a look at nationalist movements in general, they can all be thus dissected. Instead of advocating a programme of dissecting and moralizing, our programme ought to be to try to understand how this integration changes the circumstances of life for people in the contemporary Sami community. One focus is to look at the way people produce *meaning* in the context of what is happening to them and the society surrounding them. We know that processes of integration do not take place without conflicts and confrontations. Processes like these are not linear in time and space as may be the impression we get through short historical introductions and contextualisations like the one I have given here. In the context of Sami – Norwegian relations, the conflicts and confrontations have increased in relation to the majority society as well as inside the Sami community, and have unfolded more openly and consistently than before. Ingold's text could have highlighted and given us a more thorough understanding of the role of external factors in changing the Skolt Samis lifesituation for good or for worse. His text might also have helped us understand the processes of shaping a national Sami identity. Being a Sami is nomore a fixed state of mind than being a French-Canadian or a Scandinavian.

At the time being I am trying to understand how the processes of integration which I have sketched here have changed the life situation for people in a specific Sami community. Despite efforts from the State, which has clearly meant material and cultural progress – negative effects such as high rates of unemployment, violence and drug abuse we hear about from other northern areas, are in no way so prominent here, – and despite the fact that ethnic incorporation has created possibilities for many to cope with their personal dilemmas concerning ethnic identity management, we still witness people having difficulties coming to terms with their ethnic identity in actual life. How do I go about being a Sami in the modern world?

My focus is to try to identify the *systems of meaning* people produce regarding this process of national integration and ethnic incorporation. What I hear, then, is a *discourse* about what it means to be a Sami in the modern world. Can you be a Sami, who are we, and how shall I be one? However, this debate is seldom explicitly about "how to be a Sami in the modern world". The debate is more implicit, carried on in the discourse of everyday life – in discussions, through conflicts of opinion, around themes and questions of life style. These discussions sometimes engage whole villages or towns so much that they write in the local newspaper, summon mass meetings, bring a case to the municipal council or write a resolution to the government. Just as frequently, we hear this debate around the kitchen table, in the local bar, at the work place or in a poem.

I am going to present two examples of this discourse. The first one is a resolution sent to the government as an expression of opposition towards both the establishment of the Sami Commission and the commissions's proposal regarding new principles of government policy towards the Sami. Because it was approved at Easter, 1960, the name given to this resolution is the "Easter Resolution of 1960". The other example is a poem called "Sami Women" written to a Sami women's seminar in 1985. The poem asks who the real Sami woman is.

The Easter Resolution of 1960

When the Sami Commission gave its report in 1959, it stressed, as I mentioned before, stressed the importance of mutual inter-ethnic respect. Using today's concepts we would say that the commission advocated a multicultural society or ethnic pluralism. It also stressed, as may be recalled, that there had to be a basic mutual respect if not only individual Sami but the Sami as a community were to be able to grow into and take part in the welfare state. Without this basic respect the economic and social problems in the Sami community could not be solved satisfactorily. The most provocative proposal in the commission's report was a proposal to consolidate a Sami territory, i.e. a geographically defined Sami region where the Sami language would be privileged in schools as well as in the administration. Qualified Sami were to be given priority to jobs in the administration and non-Sami would be required to learn the language. The region was also to be a juridical unity by being a separate *Sorenskriveri*, a district magistrate and police district. Another proposal was to establish a Sami national advisory board.

These proposals from the commission provoked a debate in formal as well as informal fora in the Sami core area. In one village the debate became very hot. Here a mass meeting (as they called it themselves) was summoned, and a resolution passed and sent to the government. The meeting opposed the appointment of a Sami commission as such. They stressed that they felt they were one with the rest of the population in the country, and they had "neither asked for nor wished any special rights or plights compared to the rest of the inhabitants in Norway." They did, however, support the commission in its proposal to develop the region economically, as for instance develop the agriculture, reindeer management or road constructions; – i.e. the welfare-political goals which had been set up for the North. One of the statements in the resolution had to do with the proposal to establish a separate Sami administrative and juridical region. On this point the mass meeting stated:

"We will therefore by all means oppose any initiative which has as its aim to keep the Sami population in a separately organised society in inner-Finnmark. ... We strongly oppose all initiatives that will have as a result the establishment of separate bodies for the Sami, and we request that the Sami council for Finnmark be dissolved. We have learned that such bodies are used against our wishes and interests, and we find such guardianship hurting as well as unnecessary."
(St. meld. nr. 21 (1962-63) p. 50)

As to the language situation, the mass meeting was of the opinion that the commission's proposal was not in accordance with the reality in which the Sami found themselves after World War II. Their opinion was that the proposal from the Sami Commission would be

"... a fatal step back which would reverse the development and create a lot of difficulties for our youths and their future existence.

As everybody else we also love our mother tongue. But we have to realize that we cannot and do not want to stop the development which today goes in the direction of more Norwegian even in the Sami homes." (op.cit. p. 50)

The debate provoked by the Sami Commission was a discourse about whether or not you could be a Sami in a modern world. The Sami Commission was of the opinion that this was possible, assuming that the State gave both groups good conditons for growth and existence. The mass meeting's view was that Sami language and culture would not survive, but on the contrary, was a hindrance in the modern society everybody wished to take part in. Nothing could stop the development, and development meant economic welfare. The choice was *either* ethnic identity *or* increasing standard of living.

In retrospect we know that the possibilities for being a Sami – also in the modern world Samiland has become a part of – has changed dramatically. In today's Sami society the discourse is no longer *whether* you can be a Sami, but *how*. In the 70s, the high peak of the ethnic incorporation process, there was little room for doubt at least within the ethnopolitical movement, when it came to questions of who were the Sami and how should you be a Sami in the modern world. The difference between "us" and "them", between Sami and Norwegians, was clear. Old myths and stereotypes were restored and reproduced. Resolutions like the preceding one, was snorted at and understood either as an expression that the signers were definitively assimilated or they were being used in the political game of local Norwegian politicians. The more general understanding, that this resolution in fact expressed a personal experience of these individuals of having failed in the Norwegian society, creating a fear that their children were to go through the same, was not there during the first years of establishing a Sami nation and a new Sami self-awareness. One who dared to express the personal doubts and dilemmas she was constantly experiencing – despite all the nice declarations about equality, the right to be a Sami, the importance of the language as the key to the culture –

was the singer Mari Boine Persen. This was, I believe, the reason for her popularity outside the "congregation" of ethnopoliticians. She asked people to understand attitudes such as those expressed in the above resolution; - "remember they have lived long, and have experienced other conditions".

Obviously, more is needed than a Sami singer asking for understanding and contextualization, and the discource about *how* to be a Sami is still going on as we will see in this poem by Inga Ravna Eira:

Sami Women

Anne claims she is a reindeer-herders daughter
but she is studying
and she cannot even make reindeer-skin boots.

Biret is the wife of a reindeer herder
but she doesn't have any sons.

Ristin is also the wife of a reindeer herder
but she is working in a store.
Who then makes reindeerskin boots for her husband?

Elle is also the wife of a reindeer herder.
She has two grown-up sons
and therefore no help with the handicraft work.

Tone is also the wife of a reindeer herder
but she is a Norwegian.
She does handicraft, but doesn't speak the language.

Sara claims she is a Sami
talks the language
but is married to a Norwegian.

Alehtta also claims she is a Sami
but she doesn't live in the Sami core area.

Inga also claims she is a Sami
but she doen't wear Sami clothes.

Gutnil is also trying to be a Sami
but she doesn't speak the language.
Her mother is a Norwegian.

Gadja also claims she is a Sami
but she doesn't talk the real Sami language.

Marja also claims she is a Sami
but she doesn't behave like a Sami ought to.

And I am wondering
how is
the real Sami woman.

(Eira 1989. Translation by Stordahl)

The poem points to processes of new differentiating mechanisms in the Sami community, and all the questions these provoke about how the real Sami woman is.

What the author does in this poem is to make visible the everyday discussions that take place about "how to be a Sami in the modern world". She has perceived and put words to the many new subjects and relationships people in today's Sami society has to cope with in their lives. She questions the *gender relationship* when she asks who is going to make reindeerskin boots to Ristins husband since she is working at the general store, when she asks who can help Elle with the sewing since she has only got sons, or when she indicates that Biret, even though she is a reindeer herder's wife, doesn't have any sons. She deals with the often conflicting *inter-ethnic relations* when she points to the fact that Sara is married to a Norwegian, Gutnil doesn't speak the Sami language because her mother is a Norwegian, or that Tone actually is Norwegian even though she is married to a reindeer herder. She deals with the *internal cultural variation* when she doubts the Sami-ness of Alehtta since she isn't living in the so-called Sami core area. She deals with *language* when she points to the fact that Gadja doesn't speak the correct Sami dialect. She deals with *clothing styles* when she points to Inga who does not wear Sami clothes.

The author, on the one hand, makes visible the many role-combinations that are available in today's Sami community, while on the other hand, she expresses and transmits the scepticism that is felt towards such combinations. Throughout the poem she calls in question each woman's self-awareness. Is it possible to combine her new gender role, mother role or professional role with her ethnic identity. This scepticism and doubt, I will claim, is a keynote in today's Sami community, something that everybody is confronted with and experience. There is no hiding place for anyone, as the poem also tells us. There is always something you can put your finger on and make dubious. The potential to offend, dishonour, throw suspicion on, mock at, shut the mouth on somebody, is enormous! At the same time such actions easily fall back on yourself because the community is not bigger than people know "what kind of a person you are". Someone knows something about your kind while others remember statements you made in you childhood or at school which they claim do not coincide with what you stand for today, therefore making you suspect as a Sami person. And everyone is the carrier of an ethnohistory full of personal defeats, because everyday life, when it runs normally, is Norwegian, even in Samiland today. The Sami way of life or looking at things are still a never ending struggle for the definition of reality. A fight, I will claim, that takes place even over the smallest everyday details; – on everything from matters of clothing style and style of housing to questions concerning the establishment of a Sami representative body. These real-life conditions make an open self-presentation difficult, for some almost insurmountable, even in a community predominantly Sami and even if the supralocal (majority) context is one where positive discrimination is an acknowledged principle (see The Sami Rights Commission's report).

The new diversity and all the new possibilities and hopes that are held out for you daily through the schools, the media, parents, politicians etc. for some people create unsolvable dilemmas. This gives rise to a broad spectre of reactions – from a feeling of pain to grieve, aggression, apathy, constraint or closed doors, if you are not able to compose new role combination that are accepted as Sami. The consequense is that individuals get stuck as to identity and self-awareness.

The two examples I have given here belong to two periods of time and refer to change as well as continuity as to the meanings people produce regarding cultural identity and self-awareness. The question today is no longer, as was the case during the 60s, *whether* you can be a Sami, but *how.* This tells us that there has been a change in Sami self-awareness. They *are* Sami. The Sami Commission's report functioned as a midwife for a more open debate on Sami identity and self-awareness. A debate that increased in strength during the 70s. Even though many were helped sorting out their personal dilemmas through participation in the ethnopolitical movement, this was not an ideal solution for everyone. To *politicize* one's ethnic identity is not something everybody dares to do or even sees as a personal solution. It is not their ethnic identity these people reject, but they feel that there is no room for other ways of expressing their identity than through involvement in ethnopolitics.

What we can learn from this is that new ideas about equality between ethnic groups and ethnic pluralism do not take root easily in a society where ethnic assymmety has been prevailing. It is a painful process the Sami community has to go through. If it is to succeed, I see no other way than to open up for an unbiased discussion about identity, culture and self-awareness.

References

Eidheim, Harald 1971. *Aspects of the Lappish Minority Situation.* Universitetsforlaget

Eira, Inga Ravna 1989. Moalke Bàlgàt. In: *Vars, Nilsen og Eira, Savdnjiluvvon Nagir.* Davvi Media a/s.

Ingold, Tim 1976. *The Skolt Lapps Today.* Cambridge University Press.

Innstilling fra Komiteen til å utrede samespørsmål (Samekomiteen)

Minde, Henry 1980. Samebevegelsen, Det norske arbeiderparti og samiske rettigheter. In: *Thuen, T. (red.), Samene – urbefolkning og minoritet.* Universitetsforlaget.

NOU 1984. *Om samenes rettsstilling i Norge* (Sami Rights Commission)

St. meld. nr. 21 1962-63. *Om kulturelle og økonomiske tiltak av særlig interesse for den samiske befolkning.*

Aarseth, Bjørn 1978. Samekomiteen av 1956. In: *Kultur på karrig jord.* Festskrift til Asbjørn Nesheim. Norsk Folkemuseum.

Violence, Language and Politics:

Nationalism in Northern Ireland and Wales

Richard Jenkins

ABSTRACT

In this paper the nationalist political movements of two peripheral regions of the United Kingdom, Wales and Northern Ireland, are compared. In Wales the primary nationalist objectives are the preservation and promotion of a Welsh culture and way of life, as crystallised in the Welsh language. In Northern Ireland, those objectives are the reunification of Ireland and the ejection of the British state. Legitimate political action for Welsh nationalism is largely non-violent and constitutional; in Northern Ireland, armed struggle has been under way for some time. These latter differences are a reflection of different regional histories of incorporation into the British state. The paper advances two arguments. Firstly, that in analysing nationalist political movements, specific histories of state formation and political incorporation are likely to be of central importance in addition to cultural and economic factors. Second, legitimate means vary between nationalist movements – in reflection of their different relationships to the relevant metropolitan state – to such an extent that it may be more useful to talk about nationalisms rather than nationalism.

With respect to the relationship between localities and their regional or national arenas and institutions, one of the most significant dimensions of social identity is ethnicity. In the modern world, one of the most important aspects of ethnicity is nationalism, the expression and organisation of the political claim to territory and to self-determination. In this paper, I intend to address two questions. First, how are we to understand the differences between nationalism in two regions of the United Kingdom, Northern Ireland and Wales, the one a "province", the other a "principality"? Second, what are the implications of these differences, and our understanding of them, for social science debates about nationalism?

Northern Ireland and Wales: an Introduction[1]

The most obvious difference between the two territories in question is that, whilst Wales is part of the British mainland (sharing a land border with England), Northern Ireland is separated from that mainland by sea, sharing a land border with the Republic of Ireland. This is not simply a physical difference, it symbolises a more significant political reality. Wales forms a political unity with England, and England and Wales – one sometimes feels that this ought to be expressable as one word – with Scotland constitute the (relatively) ancient kingdom of Great Britain. Northern Ireland, however, as a consequence of the political settlement of the "Irish problem" in 1921, lies outside this structure – it is the United Kingdom of Great Britain *and* Northern Ireland.

There are nonetheless some things in common. Both are relatively small: Wales, with an area of 20,766 square kilometres, had a population of 2.86 million in 1988; for Northern Ireland the equivalent figures are 14,147 square kilometres and 1.58 million, yielding relative population densities of 137.6 and 111.6 persons/km². Both have mixed urban-industrial and rural agricultural economies, although the industrial area of south Wales is larger and more populous than the equivalent greater Belfast area of Northern Ireland. Northern Ireland is, however, significantly more economically disadvantaged than Wales; in January 1990 their respective unemployment rates were 6.9 per cent for Wales and 14.4 per cent for Northern Ireland, the latter being the highest of any UK region (Central Statistical Office 1990). There are a number of other basic differences which should be mentioned here. For example, as already mentioned, whilst Wales participates fully and securely in British parliamentary democracy, Northern Ireland's constitutional position is more ambiguous in at least two respects. First, although successive British governments have reiterated their support for the Province's place within the UK, this support is explicitly conditional upon a majority of the Northern Ireland population wishing to maintain this status quo. Second, the Anglo-Irish Agreement of 1985 allows the government of the Republic of Ireland a formal consultative role in the internal affairs and administration of the Province.

Northern Ireland is, therefore, a more loosely incorporated member of the federal United Kingdom state than is Wales.

The next important difference which is relevant to this discussion is the ethnic composition of their populations. Northern Ireland, as is well known, is shared by two mutually antagonistic ethnic populations: Catholics, the descendents of the original Irish population, and Protestants, who displaced that original population during the plantation of the late sixteenth and early seventeenth centuries. This was a deliberate attempt by the British government to pacify the turbulent north of Ireland by partly replacing the indigenous Irish with English and Scottish settlers. The Plantation created two ethnicities in conflict, whose existence continues to be the central structuring feature of Northern Irish society today (Jenkins 1984).

In Wales, the situation is more complex and less conflictual. In terms of the relevance of recent history, major immigration began in the nineteenth century as a consequence of the industrialisation of the south Wales coal valleys. Labour was drawn in from elsewhere in Britain, from Ireland and from as far afield as Spain and Italy. Partly because many people from rural Wales shared in the experience of immigration to the valleys, partly because of the role of the organised labour movement in forging a new, distinctly working-class, communal life in south Wales, and partly because the new migrants had to assimilate culturally in order to work (many, for example, learning to speak Welsh), sharp and conflictual ethnic differentiation did not occur, although the resultant distance between North Walians and South Walians should not be underestimated. The point is that, over successive generations, an authentically Welsh population now lives in south Wales, albeit with a diversity of antecedents. More recent has been a wave of immigration in the last two decades of affluent outsiders – typically monoglot English speakers – into rural, Welsh speaking, areas of north and west Wales (Day 1989; Symonds 1990). This has sown the seeds of considerable conflict, something to which I shall return, but it is unlikely to produce anything resembling the Northern Irish situation in terms of substantial, mutually hostile ethnic blocs.

The final difference between the two territories is the history and nature of their nationalist political movements. As someone who grew up in Northern Ireland and who moved, eventually, to Wales, one of the first differences which I noticed was in the rhetorical and actual politics of nationalism. In Northern Ireland, the nationalist objective is the re-unification of the island; since the late 'sixties and intermittently before that, the most important means to this end has been armed struggle. In Wales, the defence and promotion of Welsh culture – symbolised most sharply by the Welsh language – is the dominant item on the nationalist agenda, with some form of devolved self-government coming a poor second. The legitimate tactics for achieving these goals in Wales are constitutional democratic politics and a limited degree of direct action and protest. Since means and ends are never easily distinguishable in politics – and this is, as I shall discuss, perhaps peculiarly the case with nationalism – these differences have led me to question the degree to which the two nationalist movements, in Northern Ireland and in Wales, can be regarded as even *varieties* of the same phenomenon.

The violence of politics

At the level of the strikingly obvious, Northern Ireland is different from Wales in that it has, for more than twenty years, been the site of a complex and bloody struggle among various armed ethnic movements and the British state (Rowthorne and Wayne 1988; Whyte 1990). More than two thousand people have been killed during this period, and this provides the necessary context for understanding what follows: a discussion of attitudes towards violence as a political *means* on the part of those who espouse nationalist political *ends*. Among the Catholic public elite in Northern Ireland there is a broad spectrum of opinion concerning the role and acceptability of violence. The hierarchy of the Roman Catholic Church, the denominational community of the nationalist section of the population, has been unequivocal in its condemnation and rejection of political violence, a stance which was underlined by the appointment in 1990 of Bishop Cahal Daly, vociferous critic of paramilitary organisations, as Primate of all Ireland. The public pronouncements of individual priests with republican or nationalist sympathies may complicate this generalisation, as does the issue of whether or not the sacraments or a religious funeral should be available to unrepentant "terrorists"[2], but the overall picture is consistent. A similar stance with respect to violence is adopted by the (overwhelmingly Catholic) Social Democratic and Labour Party (SDLP). As the political voice of constitutional nationalism, advocating the re-unification of Ireland via democratic process – presumably when either the Catholic population becomes a majority in Northern Ireland, enough of the Protestants change their mind, the British parliament has a change of heart, or, more recently, the process of European unification renders the problem solved through irrelevance – the SDLP has no choice. It *must* oppose violence, although it has a long tradition of association with various forms of non-violent extra-parliamentary action. In purely political terms it also has little choice. To embrace violence would be to render itself indistinguishable in many respects from its main rival for Catholic votes, the republican Provisional *Sinn Féin*.

The other major collective actor at this level is the

republican movement (so called because of its advocacy of a particular kind of government in the all Ireland context), specifically the Provisional Republican movement: Provisional *Sinn Féin*[3], political party, and the Provisional IRA,[4] a well armed and highly successful illegal paramilitary organisation. This dual-pronged strategy is publicly represented as "the ballot box and the Armalite", the latter being a particularly useful American assault rifle. The Provisional movement is clear in its advocacy of violence as a legitimate means of forcing British withdrawal from the Province *and* as a defensive strategy for protecting the Catholic population from the security forces and from the attacks of Protestant paramilitary organisations.

At the level of public political debate within the nationalist community, there is, therefore, a range of opinions about the legitimacy of violence. What, however, of the ordinary members of that community, the constituency to which nationalist politicians must appeal? In the north Belfast Catholic enclave studied by Frank Burton in the early 1970s (Burton 1978), support from the community for the use of violence by the Provisionals was shifting, situational and conditional. The defensive role – this was a time of vicious interpersonal sectarian attacks in this part of Belfast – was seen as legitimate; offensive violence was problematic, however. Within the area there was considerable public tension between the Catholic Church and the republican movement. By the early 'eighties, when Jeff Sluka undertook field research in Divis Flats, a Catholic area of west Belfast, this tension had increased considerably (Sluka 1989). Public support in the area for the "armed struggle" as the means of securing a united Ireland was substantial; more than half the people surveyed by Sluka expressed views of this kind. The urban nationalist community's experience of the Northern Irish "troubles", in particular specific things such as the H-Blocks hunger strike, appears to have led to increased, consolidated and less equivocal support for violence as a political option (although it must also be remembered that many people in these same communities are still led by their religious faith to a rejection of violence).

In rural communities, the research literature – typically social anthropological – suggests a rather different picture: of Catholics and Protestants continuing to interact as well as possible *despite* the "troubles", of an implicit rejection of violence, of a degree of harmony and coexistence (Buckley 1980; Bufwak 1982; Glassie 1982; Donnan and Macfarlane 1983). Given that some of the most violent areas of the province are rural – near the border – and that the IRA for a long time now has been waging an intermittent campaign in rural areas against part-time members of the security forces (who are, almost by definition, Protestant), this may seem somewhat surprising. It is perhaps in part a reflection of the locations chosen for anthropological field studies, and in part a testimony to the enduring residual power of a consensus view of the social world, derived from structural functionalism, in much anthropological thinking. My concern here is not to deny that there is some important truth in this comforting picture of country folk living their everyday lives as uneventfully as they can manage. Rather, it seems likely that the picture – particularly in the current climate – will be more complex. Certainly, recent research in County Tyrone, in a community near the border (Finn 1990; Hamilton *et al* 1990: 39-56), suggests a situation closer to that which exists in Belfast or Derry: conditional support among Catholics for the Provisional IRA's campaign and conflict between this support and Catholicism and "moderate" constitutional nationalism.

Finally, with respect to nationalist opinion in both urban and rural areas of Northern Ireland it cannot be emphasised too strongly that support for, or rejection of, the methods of the Provisional IRA (or, indeed, other smaller republican groups such as INLA, The Irish National Liberation Army) is related to enthusiasm for Irish unity in complex ways which shortage of space precludes exploring here. Nationalism does not necessarily translate into either acceptance of, or support for, violence. Nor should it be forgotten that the context within which Catholic support for violence must be understood is the violence of the state security forces and Protestant paramilitary organisations. With the benefit of hindsight, it seems clear that the present conflict in Northern Ireland has its immediate historical roots in the violent repression of the (largely Catholic) civil rights movement by the (Protestant) Stormont regime in the late 1960s. One popular image of the subsequent "troubles" which must be rejected is that of the British Army as a disinterested mediator or referee, standing between two "tribal" factions: for many years now it has been a three-cornered struggle, with an ambiguous relationship existing between the British state and Protestant "Loyalists".

Moving across the water to Wales, one of the most obvious features of Welsh nationalism is the more or less complete rejection of violence against persons. There is a sporadic history of extra-parliamentary activity in support of the nationalist political agenda, particularly by *Mudiad Amddiffyn Cymru* (MAC, Movement for the Defence of Wales) and the Free Wales Army in the 1960s (Clews 1980), and there were three deaths as a result of explosions at the time of the Investiture of the Prince of Wales in 1969. However, there is no evidence to suggest that deliberate violence against English people or their representatives *as such* (and this is, I recognise, a somewhat equivocal way of discussing the matter) forms any part of this aspect of nationalist activity. The tradition of direct action has been continued in the 1980s by *Meibion Glyndŵr* (The Sons of Glyndŵr), with their incendiary campaign focused on absentee-owned second homes and the estate agents who sell them. Once again, the focus is upon attacks on property. At the time of writing, some public debate has been caused by the remarks of the poet R.S. Thomas to a meeting of *Cyfamodwyr y Cymru Rhydd* (The Covenanters of the Free Welsh), calling for a campaign of "non-violent night attacks" upon the homes of English people in Welsh-speaking districts (*The Guardian,* 17 September 1990).

Organisations such as these represent, in terms of the numbers of people involved, only a tiny element of Welsh nationalism. Nor should they be seen as representative of a wider strand of opinion, although there can be little doubt that the issue of second homes, for example, is one about which many people hold strong views and they may thus be ambiguous about the *Meibion Glyndŵr* campaign. Both *Plaid Cymru* (the parliamentary political party of Welsh nationalism) and *Cymdeithas yr Iaith Gymraeg* (the Welsh Language Society), the two main institutional expressions of Welsh nationalism, are unequivocal in their rejection of the use of violence of any kind[5]. In a recent anthropological study of nationalism in North Wales, what is striking is the *absence* of any debate about the legitimacy of violence (Davies 1989). Violence not only hardly represents an option, it is popularly rejected both on pragmatic grounds, as a likely obstruction to the movement's goals, and on moral grounds, in reflection of the strong thread of Christian pacifism which has always existed within Welsh nationalism (e.g. Evans 1973; Rees 1975). The furore aroused by R.S. Thomas's advocacy of *non*-violent direct action, referred to above, is a good indication of the depth of feeling on the issue. The overwhelming majority of the nationalist political constituency in Wales, despite the existence of considerable ambiguity about the "second homes" arson campaign, do not regard violence, particularly where life and limb are concerned, as either a sensible or a proper means to achieve their goals. It is not, certainly not *yet,* an "armed struggle".

The politics of language

Reading the previous section provides us with a clue about where to begin any comparison of the relationship between nationalism and language in Wales and Ireland. Most of the nationalist organisations in Wales have Welsh names; this is not the case in Northern Ireland, where only *Sinn Féin* adopts an Irish name, and even that derives from an earlier, all-Ireland historical context. The plain fact is that, whereas in Wales the Welsh language, despite a long-term trend of decline, remains a first language of daily use for many people, in Northern Ireland Irish is, effectively, dead.

To look at Wales first, there are a number of indicators which relate to the contemporary status of the language (Coupland and Ball 1989). Census figures, for example, suggest a decline in the number of Welsh speakers from about 930,000 in 1901 (50 per cent of the total population of Wales) to a little over ½ million (19 per cent of the population) in 1981. Towards the end of this period, and since 1981, as a result of the work of language activists and the impact of the 1967 Welsh Language Act, Welsh as a notable presence in the public domain – in official and other documents, on television and the radio and on public displays and signs of various kinds – has, however, increased in salience. In terms of its distribution, while the language remains more important in daily usage in *y fro Gymraeg,* the rural heartland of the north and west, in absolute numbers the majority of Welsh speakers now live in the industrial areas of south Wales (Davies 1990; Williams 1989).

It is not possible to produce properly comparable figures for Northern Ireland, since use of Irish is not enumerated by the Census. The last native Irish speakers passed away during the 1960s and the language now survives solely by dint of formal education and activism. Surveying the available statistics and research, one recent authority concludes that:

> "the death of native Irish in its last refuges in Northern Ireland in Rathlin, the Glens of Antrim and the Sperrin Mountains has not been balanced by any substantial accretion of effective second-language learners who have proved their ability to transmit Irish naturally or semi-naturally to their own offspring." (Hindley 1990:40)

Elsewhere (pp. 155-6) the same author cites research which suggest that less than one per cent of the population in Northern Ireland has any "complex" knowledge of Irish, with hardly anyone using it as the language of daily life in the home. More Catholic school children know French than know Irish, which serves only to emphasise the degree to which the promotion of Irish speaking in Northern Ireland has become a lost cause[6].

The contrast, therefore, is complete. Welsh, although in decline during the twentieth century, remains an important language of everyday life and there may be good grounds for qualified optimism about its future. Irish in Northern Ireland – and throughout the rest of Ireland – is, however, at best a dead or dying language, for which the best that can be hoped of is a degree of preservation.

The roots of the different trajectories of these two Celtic languages lie in earlier history, but one of the important points to recognise is that if there are grounds for guarded optimism with respect to Welsh, this is in a large part due to long-standing campaigns of activism in the present century and, indeed, earlier (Jones 1973). This activism must be seen as an integral part of the nationalist movement in Wales. It would not be over emphasising its importance to suggest that the language issue is in fact the central, uniting theme of Welsh nationalism. *Cymdeithayr Iaith Cymraeg,* the

Welsh Language Society, is one of the key institutional expressions of nationalist sentiments and ambitions (Davies 1973). It is not without significance that the two major nationalist political achievements in Wales have been the Welsh Language Act, the result in 1967 of a sustained and controversial campaign of non-violent direct action and disruption, and the establishment of the Welsh language television station, S4C, *Sianel Pedwar Cymru* or Channel Four Wales, the latter in the face of public opposition from no less a person than the then Prime Minister, Margaret Thatcher (Davies 1989: 37-58).

To further underline the centrality of culture and language in the politics of nationalism in Wales, one has only to consider the issues which are of salience at the time of writing. The first of these is the "second homes" problem, which has already been alluded to and which has been an issue for some time (Bollom 1978). The concern here is about people living outside rural, Welsh speaking areas buying up properties in these area, at what are for them low prices but which are unaffordable for many local people, for use as occasional holiday homes. The nationalist objection to this trend derives from the shortage of affordable rural housing. The price distortions which are produced in local housing markets in *y fro Gymraeg* mean that local young people have nowhere to live in their home areas. This, together with rural unemployment, produces emigration and a loss to the area of Welsh speakers. Second homes, and the estate agents who sell them, have been the targets of *Meibion Glyndŵr's* campaign of arson.

Migration and housing are at the heart of a second focus of concern: the immigration into *y fro Gymraeg* of non-Welsh speaking people, whether they be young families seeking a rural idyll and the "good life", or retired people who have sold a house in a more expensive area of the UK and bought a cheap retirement home in rural Wales (Day 1989; Symonds 1990). The arrival of relatively affluent, house-buying newcomers is a further constraint on local housing markets and the ability of locals to maintain an active presence in them. The demographic structure of whole areas also alters, with the presence of many more elderly people putting pressure on health and social provision. The younger migrants and their children alter the character of school populations. It is this which has produced the third issue of current importance: Welsh language education policies. With the shift during the 1980s in the balance of rural school populations in north and west Wales from mainly Welsh-speaking to, in some areas, mainly English-speaking, the issue of whether education should be in the medium of Welsh has provoked conflict between parents, community members and cultures. In Dyfed, for example, this has, in part, found expression in conflict within local government between the Labour Party and *Plaid Cymru*.

The important point to emphasise is that all three cases – holiday homes, immigration and education – are manifestations of the same pcoblem: the threat to Welsh culture, and its most visible and important manifestation, the language. How is Welsh culture to be maintained, let alone promoted, if the only arbiter of policy is the market, whether for labour or for houses? This is the central essence of the current nationalist political agenda and, incidentally, goes to the heart of one aspect of the difficult relationship which exists between nationalism and the Welsh labour movement: there is still much work to be done in constructing a satisfactory image of "real" Welshness which admits the majority who do *not* speak Welsh (Giles and Taylor 1978)[7].

Language and culture are not the *only* items on the nationalist agenda, and self government or devolved government remains a goal, despite the defeat of the 1979 referendum on the issue (Drucker and Brown 1980). The way forward in this respect is now seen to lie within Europe, as the overall framework within which some degree of local autonomy can be achieved (Jenkins 1990; Rees 1990). These aspiration aside, however, the language, and its defence, remains the unifying framework of nationalist discourse.

In Northern Ireland, by complete contrast, the language is hardly an issue. It serves some symbolic purpose – it may be heard, for example, from the platform at the annual meeting, the *Árd Fheis*, of the Provisional movement, and there have been successful minor struggles to rename some Belfast streets in Irish – and there are many anecdotes concerning the Provisional IRA's use of Irish in radio traffic to confuse the security forces. There is also small-scale language activism (Hindley, op. cit: 156-9). However, the defence and promotion of the Irish language is peripheral – at best – to the central demands of nationalism in Northern Ireland. Irish unity, self-government and freedom from Britain are of overwhelming significance and non-negotiable. Which is not to say that culture and language are irrelevant within Irish nationalism. There is, indeed, a long history of "cultural nationalism" in Ireland (Hutchinson 1987). With its centre of gravity in Dublin, however, this slipped down the order of priorities once the Irish nation state, albeit minus the six northern counties, was established in 1923. While Irish/Gaelic culture continues to do useful service rhetorically, it is no longer central to nationalist objectives, whether they derive from north or south of the border. With the development of tourism and international economic links, culture has become more of a marketing phenomenon than a matter for struggle.

Towards an explanatory model

To sum up the discussion so far, I have compared two different constituent territories of the United Kingdom, each part of the "Celtic fringe", each institutionally integrated into the UK in different ways and to different degrees, and each possessing well-defined and -supported nationalist movements. In the case of Northern Ireland, violence is part of the "rules of engagement" with the British state; in Wales, this is emphatically not the case. In Wales, the most important political issues, which serve to unify the competing strands of nationalist opinion, are language and culture; in Northern Ireland, by contrast, these are relatively insignificant when compared to the central nationalist objective, freedom from British rule.

How to understand these differences is the primary theme of this paper, and perhaps the best place to start is with the burgeoning social science literature on nationalism. There is no space here for a comprehensive survey of this literature, so what follows is of necessity a partial (and personal) selection.

One of the most celebrated recent contributions to the debate has been Gellner's *Nations and Nationalism* (1983). In this account, nationalism, as a self-conscious political ideology concerned with the self determination of "nations", is a product of the nineteenth century rise of industrial society, with its linked requirements of cultural/linguistic homogeneity and a workforce generically educated for participation in a modern economy. Here the stress is upon the relationship between an industrial system and a literate, national "high" culture. Anderson, in his discussion of the "imagined political communities" which are nations (1983), adopts a perspective not dissimilar to Gellner's, although the emphasis here is upon industrial *capitalism* and the homogenising potential of print technologies in the creation of national self-consciousness.

One of the few authors to have examined comparatively the situation in Wales and Ireland is Hechter, in *Internal Colonialism* (1975). In that book, and more clearly in a subsequent paper on "ethnoregionalism" (Hechter and Levi 1979), Hechter relates the development of different kinds of "ethnoregional" – in this context, nationalist – movements to different forms of ethnically-structured divisions of labour. In other words, what matters is the manner in which different ethnic or national groups are incorporated into the economy and the stratification system, producing either a hierarchical or a segmented cultural division of labour (an analysis which has something in common with Horowitz's notion of ranked and unranked systems of ethnic stratification; see Horowitz 1985). In the overall economistic framework which he proposes, Hechter also acknowledges the role of cultural differentiation and the behaviour of the state in producing nationalist political movements.

Gellner, Hechter and Anderson all offer analyses in which economic factors are, in one way or another, central. Smith, by way of contrast, puts forward a model in which cultural or symbolic factors are most

important (Smith 1981; 1986). Here the emphasis is on group identification as a bundle of cultural processes, preceding nationalism as a modern ideology and, paradoxically perhaps, encouraging its continued vitality when, according to other authors (e.g. Gellner, op cit.: 110-122; Hobsbawm 1990: 163-183), its power and attraction ought to be on the wane. Kedourie's argument (1985) is even more idealistic: for him, nationalism is a political philosophy in its own right – not "a reflection of anything else" (be it economic or cultural) – with its power rooted in nineteenth century political history.

Recognising that to summarise them thus is to gloss over the fine points of these authors' arguments, on the one hand there are analyses rooted in economic factors while, on the other, culture, ideology and/or values are emphasised. There are some authors who synthesise elements of each side of the debate (e.g. Breuilly 1985). With the limited exception of Hechter, whose arguments are, for my purposes, disappointingly non-specific, they do not, however, contribute much to an understanding of the differences between nationalisms in Wales and Northern Ireland. In particular, issues such as the role of violence and the significance of language and culture seem poorly accounted for. Since these are, as I have suggested, important for our understanding of those differences, this is a major shortcoming.

The other shortcoming in this literature – and there are, once again, limited exceptions to this generalisation (e.g. Breuilly; Hechter) – is the somewhat surprising de-emphasis of the state and political action. Returning to the topic of the relationship between localities and their regional or national institutional contexts, I want to argue that, in addition to economic and cultural factors, politics and the state, particularly long-term processes of state formation, must be placed at the centre of attempts to understand nationalism. In particular, drawing on Weber's classic discussion of the rise and nature of the nation-state (1978: 54-56, 901-926) and Giddens' more recent discussion of the importance of "internal pacification" in state formation (1985: 172-197), I propose to look at two linked historical processes which may allow us to begin to answer the first of the questions posed at the beginning of the paper: (1) the history of the incorporation of each territory, Wales and Northern Ireland, into the United Kingdom state, and (2) the degree to which the state has successfully monopolised violence in each territory (and, as a consequence, the degree to which violence has been removed from the political domain).

Northern Ireland and Wales compared (again)

To look first at processes of state integration, Wales was finally politically united with England in 1536, by the Act of Union. Before that, integration, built upon the accession of the Welsh Tudor dynasty to the English throne following Henry Tudor's victory at the battle of Bosworth Field in 1485, had been effective if not constitutionally formalised. Before that again, the last major Welsh rebel against Anglo-Norman suzerainty, Owain Glyndŵr had been defeated in 1408, and before that again, Edward I had subdued the kingdoms of Gwynedd and Deheubarth by 1283. Not only is the political unity of England and Wales long-standing, but it is legitimated by the role of the Tudors in the establishment of the modern English state and by their contribution to modern images of the continuity and the role of the monarchy. The use of the title Prince of Wales for the male heir to the throne is indicative of the perceived stability of the Union.

There have, it is true, been some changes in the twentieth century. A range of specifically Welsh public and governmental agencies have come into being, the most important being the Welsh Office, created in 1964 and run by the Secretary of State for Wales, a ministerial post of cabinet rank. Barry Jones (1988) has argued, however, that the degree of autonomy from London which these institutions possess is often limited, as is the extent to which they have penetrated and become a legitimate part of Welsh society. Despite some degree of local institutional specialisation, the unity of England and Wales remains the established and taken-for-granted political order for most Welsh people.

Northern Ireland, however, is a wholly different case. Apart from the period between 1800 and 1921, Ireland has never been an integral part of the British polity. Irish history since the arrival of the Normans in 1169 has been a history of more or less violent attempts to impose or maintain British control, and more or less violent resistance to that control. The north of the island proved particularly obdurate and remained the heart of Gaelic Irish culture; so much so that in the sixteenth century the English adopted a policy of dispossessing the indigenous (Catholic) Irish population by force, replacing them with immigrant (Protestant) Scottish and English settlers. As was argued earlier, this settlement, the Plantation, is the reason why there are in Northern Ireland today two mutually antagonistic ethnic populations, identified religiously as Catholic and Protestant.

The province of Northern Ireland was established as part of the United Kingdom in 1921, in reflection of the, often violently expressed, determination of the Protestant population not to join the rest of Ireland in its new freedom from British rule. Many Catholics in the north, perhaps the majority, did not accept the legitimacy of the partition of the island. Between 1921 and 1972 the province was a semi-independent member of the federal United Kingdom with its own parliament, governing its internal affairs largely in the inter-

ests of the Protestants. Following the imposition in 1972, as a result of renewed serious violence, of direct rule from London, the province remained substantially apart from the rest of the UK. It is legislatively distinct, it has completely different systems of local government and public service administration, and its membership of the UK is constitutionally strictly conditional upon the continued assent to the status quo of a numerical majority of the population. There is nothing conditional about the unity of the rest of the kingdom. What is more, since the Anglo-Irish Agreement of 1985, there is a formally defined – although locally contentious – consultative role for the government of the Republic of Ireland in the Province's affairs.

With respect to state integration, therefore, whereas Wales could be described as strongly and securely a part of the United Kingdom, completely tied in to the legislative and administrative order, Northern Ireland is a peripheral and weakly integrated member of the UK. This state of affairs is, as one might expect, relevant to the issue of the state's monopolisation of violence. In Wales, following Glyndŵr's defeat in 1408, the state monopolisation of violence has been more or less total. Such major interruptions of the state's capacity to guarantee public order as there were – the Civil War, for example – were conflicts within the state of England and Wales, the legitimacy of which was not in doubt. In the nineteenth century there was class conflict, the Rebecca Riots of 1842-43 and the earlier Chartist rising in Newport, for example, but this was largely similar to contemporary events in England; there was no peculiarly *Welsh* problem of public order. As a consequence, from the mid-nineteenth century onwards the domain of political activity has been largely governed by rules which do not allow for violence; the military has long since withdrawn from politics, in Wales as in England.

Northern Ireland, once again, is different. In Ireland violence has *never* been successfully monopolised by the state. Every century since the first arrival of the Normans has been marked by uprisings against the English or British state. More to the point, the state has been ethnically partisan. After 1921 it only managed to achieve a partial monopolisation of violence in Northern Ireland by authorising informal Protestant violence in the shape of a local, paramilitary police force. For fifty years, the state in Northern Ireland was, effectively, the Protestant population, and its rule was based on coercion.

Violence remains, therefore, a key item in the repertoire of political options in Northern Ireland; it is part of the rules of the political game. All three parties to the current situation – Protestants, Catholics and the British state – depend upon violence, whether explicitly or implicitly, as the means to their particular ends.

Which brings us, once again following Weber, to an important distinction, that between *power* and *authority* (see Smith 1960: 15-33). Power is basically the capacity to make people do what one wants them to do, most typically through the use of coercion; authority is the legitimate and delegated right to command obedience. Power is rooted, ultimately, in the use of force, authority in the law and legality. In Wales, for a very long time now, the state has been legitimate and so has its authority. Most of the spectrum of nationalist politics operates within the framework of this *overall* legitimacy. In Northern Ireland, however, the legitimacy of the state is a problem for the Catholic nationalist population (since 1972, and direct rule, this has also been the case for many Protestants). Politics are a matter of power rather than authority, at least with respect to the basic questions of the nature, form and functions of the state, and violence is one of the accepted possibilities with respect to political action.

But what about the issues of culture and language? Once again, the key to understanding the situation is the history of the territory's integration into the state (although here my analysis may be a little more contentious). Wales gave up armed struggle against England very early in its history. As a consequence, it was subject to a less direct and repressive form of control and government than either Ireland or Scotland. This may have created the social and economic space within which Welsh language and culture – not being sufficiently dangerous, perhaps – could survive. Whereas in Ireland and Scotland, indigenous culture and the Gaelic languages became identified with Catholicism in post-reformation geo-political struggles, in Wales the language eventually became identified with Protestant Nonconformity. This may have been a threat to the established Church, but it was not a threat to the state. During the nineteenth century, and this once again is a reflection of the two countries' differing relationships to the central state, there was the Great Famine in Ireland – which, with benefit of hindsight, was probably the biggest single blow to Gaelic Irish culture – and massive industrialisation in South Wales, something which brought a late flowering of Welsh culture to the coal valleys. Just as the Famine would have been unthinkable in Wales, so was industrialisation out of the question for the south and west of Ireland.

The north of Ireland was, by the nineteenth century, already thoroughly Anglicised. The Plantation, two centuries earlier, had seen to that. Throughout Ireland, the state's control was more repressive and more severe than anywhere on the mainland. In the north, where industrialisation did occur – although not on the scale of south Wales – it was largely in Belfast and its hinterland. The Irish language did not survive the migration to the eastern seaboard in search of employment. There was neither the social nor the economic

space available to facilitate any late recovery for a language and a culture which had been marginalised (at best) by the Plantation, undermined by penal laws during the eighteenth century and dealt a final blow by famine and social dislocation in the nineteenth century.

The suggestion is, therefore, that the conditions which facilitate the survival of a minority language are bound up with the way in which the linguistic homeland becomes integrated into the central state. Further, part of the structure of integration will be mechanisms and institutions of social control – some of these may be specifically aimed at discouraging the indigenous language and culture. This latter occurred more severely in Ireland than in Wales.

Comparing the nationalist movements of Wales and Northern Ireland, it is clear that the differences between them with respect to their capacity for the use of violence and their emphasis upon language and culture are, in large part, a reflection of the history of each territory's integration into the British state. Where the language of a peripheral territory has survived it is, *ipso facto,* likely to be a substantial item on the political agenda of any nationalist movement; where it has not survived in any major way, it is unlikely to be a focus for popular support. Similarly, where the process of internal pacification, which Giddens has characterised as a central aspect of modern nation-state formation, has been successfully extended to the periphery, violence is unlikely to form part of the nationalist struggle. Where violence remains part of the array of political possibilities, it will, necessarily almost, be used.

Conclusion

There are a number of things to be said in closing. First, nationalist movements are not social phenomena which can be looked at in isolation. Their character and development, whether they be the political expression of peripheral minority peoples or dominant metropolitan populations, is inextricably bound up with the processes of modern nation-state formation. In discussions of local-level identities and movements which are, in whatever sense, definable as nationalist, it is, therefore, not possible to limit the scope of analysis to that local level. Nor is it possible to ignore an often substantial history of contact and state integration. Nationalist movements are not things unto themselves, and their history is shared with other peoples and places within a context of metropolitan expansion, power and the struggle for control.

Second, lest I be misunderstood, while it has been my intention to re-emphasise the politics of state formation, it is no part of my argument to suggest that economic and cultural explanations of nationalism do not have their place. As I hope my comparison of

Northern Ireland and Wales has illustrated, I do not think that this is the case. What I am suggesting is that any comprehensive analytical account of nationalism must take account, within an appropriately historical framework, of political, cultural *and* economic factors. Anything else will be partial (and probably in both senses of that word). As an example of a properly rounded discussion of nationalism, the reader should perhaps look at O'Sullivan See's comparison of Northern Ireland and Quebec (1986).

Finally, my analysis has some further implications for social science debates about nationalism[8]. The question must be asked: to what extent are we actually talking about the same phenomenon in Wales and Northern Ireland? Here the issue of the legitimacy of the central state is central. The fact that each "nationalist" movement has recourse to an essentially nineteenth century rhetoric of self-determination does not make them the same thing (and much the same could, I suspect, be said about the various nationalisms which have reappeared in eastern and central Europe and the Balkans). In Wales the struggle is over culture and language and the state is, for the overwhelming majority of the "nationalist" population, a legitimate institution albeit one whose reform they seek. In Northern Ireland, the struggle, for most nationalists, is about the state itself. At the least, they seek its complete transformation, at the most, its replacement by an authentically Irish government. The state's legitimacy – which is, after all, at the heart of the political philosophy of nationalism – is wholly different in each case. How sensible is it, therefore, to continue to subsume each under the same conceptual umbrella? It is perhaps time that we began to unpack the notion of "nationalism", even going so far perhaps as to question whether or not it remains a useful analytical concept at all. The fact that so many academic writers on the subject have confidently predicted its demise, only to be contradicted by the unravelling of the geo-political framework of the cold war in Europe, is a further argument in favour of such an approach. Nationalism is dead, long live nationalisms?

Acknowledgments. This paper has benefited enormously from its discussion at the conference on "Local organization, cultural identity and national integration", held at Aarhus University in October 1990, and from discussions with Hywel Davies. It has benefited most, however, from the encouragement and criticism of Charlotte Aull Davies, any acknowledgment to whom would be inadequate.

Notes

1. As befits a paper of this length, this is a necessarily superficial discussion. I have tried to walk a delicate line between not stating the obvious and saying enough to allow readers unfamiliar with Wales and Northern Ireland to understand the comparison.

By way of a *caveat,* the following topics have been left largely undiscussed due to constraints of space: the interaction between religion and nationalism, the peculiar and ambivalent position of Northern Irish Protestants with respect to the British state, the equally ambiguous position of the non-Welsh speaking Welsh, the international dimensions of each situation (see Guelke 1988; Jenkins 1990) and the relationship, particularly in Northern Ireland, between nationalism and republicanism. These would all deserve attention in a longer discussion.

2. The word is placed in inverted commas in order to draw attention to its function in the political rhetoric of the conflict.
3. *Sinn Féin,* which may be translated as "Ourselves", was originally a nationalist movement of the early years of the twentieth century.
4. IRA stands for Irish Republican Army.
5. Both, however, have a history of the use of non-violent, extra parliamentary direct action.
6. Something similar, if slightly less emphatic, could also be said about the status of Irish in the Republic of Ireland (Hindley 1990: 159-160).
7. "The issue of language has ... given rise from the early part of this century down to the present to a crisis in identity among the people of Wales ... it should be recognised that English-speaking Welshmen spiritedly and justifiably counter that, lack of Welsh notwithstanding, they, too, are a distinctive "Welsh" people, possessed of characteristics which separate them from their English, Scottish and Irish neighbours. For them, it is their separate history, instinctive radicalism in religion and politics, contempt for social pretentiousness, personal warmth and exuberance, sociability, love of music and near obsession with rugby which mark them out as Welshmen." (Howell and Baber 1990: 354)
8. The discussion would also suggest that, whatever the cultural and linguistic similarities which exist between the Celtic peoples of the European maritime periphery, their different histories of incorporation into the relevant metropolitan nation states (i.e. the UK and France) will discourage the emergence of the pan-Celtic nationalist movement proposed by Berresford Ellis (1985).

References

Anderson, B. 1983. *Imagined Communities: Reflections on the Origin and Spread of Nationalism,* London: Verso.

Beresford Ellis, P. 1985. *The Celtic Revolution: A Study in Anti Imperialism,* Talybont: Y Lolfa.

Bollom, C. 1978, "Attitudes towards second homes in rural Wales", in G. Williams (ed.) *Social and Cultural Change in Contemporary Wales,* Routledge and Kegan Paul.

Breuilly, J. 1985. *Nationalism and the State,* Manchester: Manchester University Press.

Buckley, A.D. 1982. *A Gentle People: A Study of a Peaceful Community,* Cultra: Ulster Folk and Transport Museum.

Bufwack, M. S. 1982. *Village Without Violence,* Cambridge, Mass.: Schenkman.

Burton, F. 1978. *The Politics of Legitimacy: Struggles in a Belfast Community,* London: Routledge and Kegan Paul.

Central Statistical Office, 1990. *Regional Trends 25,* London: Her Majesty's Stationery Office.

Clews, R. 1980. *To Dream of Freedom: The Struggle of M.A.C. and the Free Wales Army,* Talybont: Y Lolfa.

Coupland, N. and **Ball, M.J.** 1990. "Welsh and English in contemporary Wales: Sociolinguistic issues", *Contemporary Wales,* vol.3, pp.7-40.

Davies, C.A. 1989. *Welsh Nationalism in the Twentieth Century: The Ethnic Option and the Modern State,* New York: Praeger.
1990. "Language and Nation", in R. Jenkins and A. Edwards (eds.), *One Step Forward? South and West Wales Towards the Year 2000,* Llandysul: Gomer.

Davies, C. 1973. "Cymdeithas yr Iaith Cymraeg", in M. Stephens (ed.), *The Welsh Language Today,* Llandysul: Gomer.

Day, G. 1989. 'A Million on the Move'?: population change and rural Wales", *Contemporary Wales,* vol.3, pp. 137-159.

Donnan, H. and **G. Macfarlane** 1983. "Informal social organisation", in J. Darby (ed.), *Northern Ireland: The Background to the Conflict,* Belfast: Appletree Press.

Drucker, H.M. and G. Brown 1980. *The Politics of Nationalism and Devolution,* London: Longman.

Evans, G. 1973, *Non-violent Nationalism,* New Malden: Fellowship of Reconciliation.

Finn, A. 1990. *Perceptions of the Northern Ireland Conflict in a Border Community,* MPhil. Thesis, University of Ulster.

Gellner, E. 1983. *Nations and Nationalism,* Oxford: Blackwell.

Giddens, A. 1985. *The Nation-State and Violence,* Cambridge:Polity.

Giles, H. and D.M. Taylor 1978, "National identity in south Wales: Some preliminary data", in G. Williams (ed.), *Social and Cultural Change in Contemporary Wales,* London: Routledge and Kegan Paul.

Glassie, H. 1982. *Passing the Time in Ballymenone,* Philadelphia: University of Pennsylvania Press.

Guelke, A. 1988. *Northern Ireland: The International Perspective,* Dublin: Gill and Macmillan.

Hamilton, A., C. McCartney, T. Anderson and A. Finn 1990. *Violence and Communities: The Impact of Political Violence in Northern Ireland on Intra-Community, Inter-Community and Community-State Relationships,* Coleraine: Centre for the Study of Conflict.

Hechter, M. 1975. *Internal Colonialism: The Celtic Fringe in British National Development, 1536-1966,* London: Routledge and Kegan Paul.

Hechter, M. and M. Levi 1979. "The comparative analysis of ethno-regional movements", *Ethnic and Racial Studies,* vol.2, pp. 260-274.

Hindley, R. 1990. *The Death of the Irish Language: A Qualified Obituary,* London: Routledge.

Hobsbawm, E.J. 1990. *Nations and Nationalism since 1780: Programme, Myth, Reality,* Cambridge: Cambridge University Press.

Horowitz, D.L. 1985. *Ethnic Groups in Conflict,* Berkeley: University of California Press.

Howell, D.W. and C. Baber 1990. "Wales", in F.M.L. Thompson (ed.), *The Cambridge Social History of Britain 1750-1950, Volume I: Regions and Communities,* Cambridge: Cambridge University Press.

Hutchinson, J. 1987. *The Dynamics of Cultural Nationalism: The Gaelic Revival and the Creation of the Irish Nation State,* London: Allen and Unwin.

Jenkins, R. 1984. "Ethnicity and the rise of capitalism in Ulster", in R. Ward and R. Jenkins (eds.), *Ethnic Communities in Business,* Cambridge: Cambridge University Press.

1990. "International Perspectives" in R. Jenkins and A. Edwards (eds.), *One Step Forward? South and West Wales Towards the Year 2000,* Llandysul: Gomer.

Jones, B. 1988. "The development of Welsh territorial institutions: Modernization theory revisited", *Contemporary Wales,* vol.2, pp.47-61.

Kedourie, E. 1985. *Nationalism,* revised edition, London: Hutchinson.

Nairn, T. 1981. *The Break-Up of Britain: Crisis and Neo-Nationalism,* second edition, London: New Left Books.

O'Sullivan See, K. 1986. *First World Nationalisms: Class and Ethnic Politics in Northern Ireland and Quebec,* Chicago: University of Chicago Press.

Rees, I.B. 1975. *The Welsh Political Tradition,* Cardiff: Plaid Cymru.

1990. "Wales Today: Nation or Market?" *Planet,* no.79, pp.56-91.

Sluka, J.A. 1989. *Hearts and Minds, Water and Fish: Support for the IRA and INLA in a Northern Irish Ghetto,* Greenwich, Conn.: JAI Press.

Smith. A.D. 1981 *The Ethnic Revival in the Modern World,* Cambridge: Cambridge University Press.

1986. *The Ethnic Origins of Nations,* Oxford: Blackwell.

Smith, M.G. 1960. *Government in Zazzau 1800-1950,* London: Oxford University Press for the International African Institute.

Symonds, A. 1990. "Migration, communities and social change", in R. Jenkins and A. Edwards (eds.), *One Step Forward? South and West Wales Towards the Year 2000,* Llandysul: Gomer.

Weber, M. 1978. *Economy and Society,* G. Roth & C. Wittich (eds.), Berkeley: University of California Press.

Whyte, J. 1990. *Interpreting Northern Ireland,* Oxford: Oxford University Press

Williams, C.H. 1989. "New domains of the Welsh language: Education, planning and the law", *Contemporary Wales,* vol.3, pp.41-76.

Property in Common, Common Property or Private Property:

Norwegian fishery management in a Sami coastal area

Ivar Bjørklund

ABSTRACT

The article adresses the relation between national fishery management and dominant scientific theories in light of the common property debate. Is it so that freedom in the commons brings ruin to all participants? The example is Sami fishing in a north Norwegian fiord, where the Sami have regarded the marine resources as a *property in common* for the local inhabitants and have developed a local marine tenure system. The Norwegian authorities however, legally defined the fiordal resources as *common property*, thus giving all Norwegians access to the fiord. Today, local fish stocks are seriously depleted and the local Sami system of resource management is no longer intact. Norwegian authorities now want to make the remaining resources *private property*, as a solution to the problems created by the former policy of open access.

The idea of this article is to adress the relation between the principles of national fisheries management in Norway and the dominant scientific theories which this management is based upon. We all know quite a few cases where political authorities have sought to legitimate their policy by reference to science. This of course, happens just as often as scientific activity is looking for political legitimation.

The story of Sami fishery management in the fiords of northern Norway is an illustrative example of how this duality works. It is also, as we will see, a story which begs a few questions about the conventional use of the so-called common property theory. This theory, which was presented by the Canadian economist Scott Gordon in a classic article in 1954 (Gordon 1954) addresses the problem of fishery resources as common property. The axiom is that nobody owns the fish that swim in the sea. According to Gordon, "everybody's property is nobody's property". And being nobody's property, means that nobody is responsible for the management of the resources. Thus, "freedom in a commons brings ruin to all" (Hardin 1968).

This theory, as a matter of fact, is the basic paradigm guiding most legal, social and biological sciences in their understanding of fishing activities in northern Norway. Their approach seem to be based upon the belief that because access to the sea is legally open to everybody, there is no incentive for the individual fisherman to be careful and responsible. According to the theory, there is nothing to be gained for an individual

restricting his fishing efforts. On the contrary, he will be punished economically, because the same total amount will be caught by others in his place.

The problem, as has been shown by Brox (1990), is that serious epistemological misconceptions are embedded in the theory of common property. On the one hand, it is used as an *analytical model* – a tool which makes it possible to study the aggregate effects of different local adaptions. On the other hand, quite a few people – especially in political and administrative positions – look on the theory as an *empirical statement* about the world. It is quite often presented as a natural law which applies in all human settings – comparable to the law of gravity, according to the example of Brox. Such use has of course given the common property theory a tremendous political impact, as for instance presented in the political rhetoric of proponents for "sustainable development".

It is this latter use of the theory which I want to take a closer look upon, because it is this use which seems to be at the basis of much political decision-making. As will be shown, the very conditions for fishing in northern Norway, are to a large extent related to the legal and political consequences which the national authorities has drawn from the common property theory.

The Sami people of northern Fenno-Scandia has historically been divided into two groups according to their different ecological adaptions. The smallest group is the reindeer-pastoralists, today approx. com-

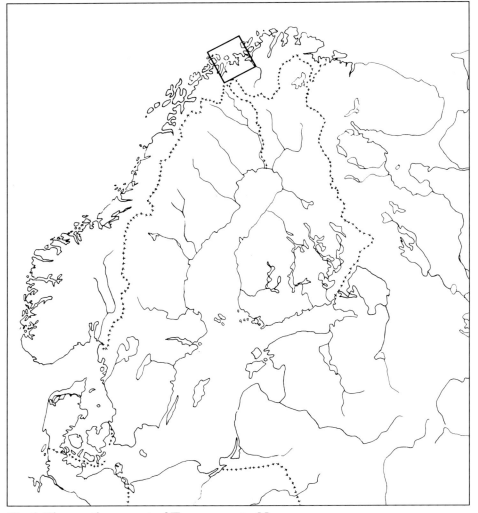

Fig. 1. The northern part of Troms county, Norway.

rive to the coast of northern Norway from the nursery grounds of the Barents Sea. Here it is caught around the Lofoten Islands and this is the largest cod fishery in the world. The Lofoten fishery has always been very important to the Norwegian economy in which, actually, today fishing represents the third most important export income.

Besides this migrating cod-stock, there seems to be a sedentary stock of cod in the fiords. But since all biological research has gone into the stock migrating from the Barents Sea, we do not have much research based knowledge about this local fiord cod. The local population though, argue that this is a stationary stock of cod, separate from the migratory Barents stock.

The cod fisheries of northern Norway then, has been of two different kind. One, and the most important in economic terms, is the seasonal fishery based on the Barents Sea stock. This takes place close to the coast of Finnmark and the Lofoten Islands and is attended by thousands of fishermen from all over northern Norway. The other is the stationary fishery taking place in the fiords all through the winter. This fishery is carried out exclusively by the local population in the fiord region, using small-scale equipment such as hand-line, long-line and gill-net.

The majority of the fiordal fishermen belong to the Sami ethnic group, and fishing has thus been a rather important income to them. Combined with subsistence husbandry and hunting for sea mammals and birds, this adaption presupposed a controlled access to fishing grounds in the fiord and to the grazing areas on shore.

Regarding the sea, the Sami seemed to define access as a property held in common by the inhabitants in the fiord. Legally, as I will comment upon later, the fiords – as well as the sea – were regarded as the property of the King (and after 1814 the State). Access to land and pasture has for the last two hundred years been legalized through the national system of property in land, according to conditions specified by the law. These conditions give any Norwegian citizen access to buy or inherit land.

prising 5000 people living in the interior of the northernmost parts of Norway, Sweden and Finland. While reindeer-herding for the last centuries has been the most important occupation, fishing and husbandry represented the main economic activities among the other Sami group, the so-called coastal Sami. These were settled along the fiords of northern Norway, and were – up to World War II – the dominant ethnic group of the northernmost part of this area. For the last 500 years, their economic adaption has consisted in commercial fishing within the fiord, subsistence husbandry, hunting and gathering.

Fishing has taken place all year round, allthough winter was the most important season due to problems in the summertime of preserving fish for commercial purposes. *Cod* has always been the most important resource, caught during the winter, dried and sold through local merchants to the European market. Together with the reindeer (*Rangifer tarandus*), the Norwegian arctic cod (*Gadus morhua*) has always been the most regular and most important resource for people living in the northernmost part of Norway. Every winter enormous amounts of spawning cod ar-

The importance to the Sami inhabitants of the fiords that access to the area be restricted, is well documented by the protests which they have on several occasions voiced against external intruders. In the 1750s they complained to the authorities that Sami reindeer herders were fishing in the fiords. A hundred years later, new complaints were sent to the king regarding Norwegian settlers occupying important grazing grounds used in common by the Sami. And from the 1950s and on, they protested strongly against the trawlers which by then had begun fishing in the fiords.

These protests tell us that the Sami living in the fiords have had a clear perception of the *exclusivity* of the resources which they exploited. Sami exploitation of resources was regarded as being based on exclusive rights held in common and obtained through centuries of use.

Now, the exploitation of all these resources has of course its managerial characteristics. In the following I will describe the way it worked as a *marine tenure system* in this century, before

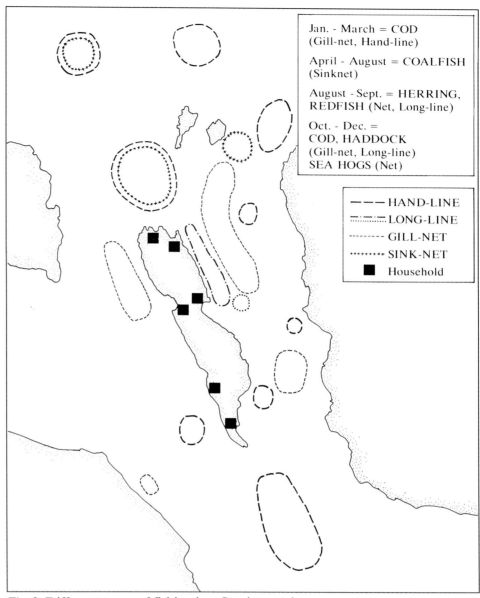

Jan. - March = COD
(Gill-net, Hand-line)

April - August = COALFISH
(Sinknet)

August - Sept. = HERRING,
REDFISH (Net, Long-line)

Oct. - Dec. =
COD, HADDOCK
(Gill-net, Long-line)
SEA HOGS (Net)

— — — HAND-LINE
·—··—··— LONG-LINE
-------- GILL-NET
········· SINK-NET
■ Household

Fig. 2. Different types of fishing in a Sami coastal area.

World War II. The example is taken from an island in a larger fiord area in the northern part of Troms county. During the 1920-30s, 6-7 households lived on this island. The technology in question during this period consisted in small sailing boats, occasionally motorized, gill-nets, hand-lines and long-lines. As fig. 2 tells us, knowledge about complex ecological interdependencies was an important condition for this kind of management system. Consequently, the inhabitants of the fiord had a vast knowledge of for instance the sea-bottom, currents, climate and the habitat and cycle of different fish species. This ecological understanding is still present in their cultural taxonomies and forms of classification. The variety of names of the seascape in this particular area, for instance, reflects an intimate knowledge of the area beneath the surface of the sea (fig.3). The comprehensive ecological knowledge which their management of marine resources was

based upon, has always been an important part of Sami cultural identity in the fiords. This knowledge, which was a necessary condition if one should harvest the resources in the fiord, could only be attained locally.

How then, was access to the marine resources regulated? There were specific rules about *who* could fish *where*. Access to the grounds for coalfish and the hideouts for herring and redfish were regarded as a property in common for all the inhabitants in the fiord. The same situation applied with respect to the catching of sea hogs, seals and sea birds. Access to areas for gill-netting and line-fishing, on the contrary, were individually defined – which means that it belonged to the individual household. These areas were more or less permanently in use during the winter season where cod and haddock represented the most important possibility of a cash income. Anyone who tried to fish

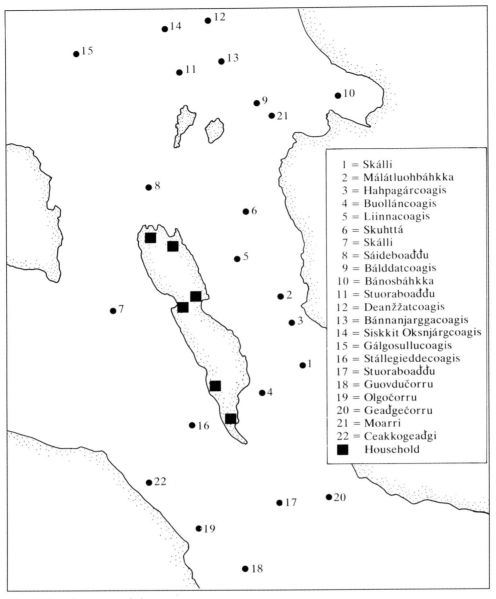

1 = Skálli
2 = Málátluohbáhkka
3 = Hahpagárcoagis
4 = Buolláncoagis
5 = Liinnacoagis
6 = Skuhttá
7 = Skálli
8 = Sáideboaddu
9 = Bálddatcoagis
10 = Bánosbáhkka
11 = Stuoraboaddu
12 = Deanžžatcoagis
13 = Bánnanjarggacoagis
14 = Siskkit Oksnjárgcoagis
15 = Gálgosullucoagis
16 = Stállegieddecoagis
17 = Stuoraboaddu
18 = Guovdučorru
19 = Olgočorru
20 = Geadgečorru
21 = Moarri
22 = Ceakkogeadgi
■ Household

Fig. 3. Sami names of the seascape.

in such an area used by other households, would be morally sanctioned.

The "key" to find any fishing-ground, is the "me" (*sami vihtat*). This is an old way of codifying and transferring the kind of ecological knowledge mentioned above. "Me" is a system of topographic coordinates which makes it possible to find the exact spot to fish while you are out at sea. By coordinating different spots ashore, you are able to find your whereabouts on the sea. This mapping system is of course well known in fishing communities all over the world. Most of these coordinates – but not all – were familiar to most men living and fishing in the area. A few of these coordinates seem to have lived a rather secret life – they were kept within the family, surrounded with a certain mystique, and consequently were not common knowledge in the fiord. These kind of coordinates thus defined access to the fishing resources in individual

terms – one had to *know* the coordinates to be able to fish.

What happened then, to the management system which I have here outlined very roughly? The answer is a comment on the relation between management policy in the Norwegian fisheries, and the scientific theory which underpins this policy – the so-called common property theory. The use of this theory in Norwegian fisheries administration is based upon the empirical assumption that the fiords – as well as the sea – is "no one's property", that is: access is in principle free for any citizen of Norway. This assumption also seems to be a basic condition both in legal (Smith 1990) and anthropological (Brox 1984) analyses of northern Norway of today. This kind of approach has made local tenure systems invisible, and thus had serious ethno-political consequences regarding marine resource management in the Sami areas. The background for this is that the state has the legal jurisdiction over the sea and the marine resources. These resources are legally defined as common property where all Norwegian citizens in principle have access.

This was the legal situation which gave a boost to the industrial fisheries just after World War II. The introduction of new technology and the opening of new markets led to the development of capital-intensive fishing. Larger boats from other parts of Norway using Danish seine or trawl began to fish in the fiords – first for herring and later for coalfish and prawn. This large-scale fishery, which totally devastated the herring stock, generated series of protests from local fishery organisations. State authorities, however, regarded this trawling as not only legal but also desirable. Small-scale fishing with low-cost technology as practised by the Sami population in the fiords, were considered old-fashioned by the economists in the Department of Fisheries. The future development was seen as synonomous with industrial trawling.

During this period – the 1960s and -70s – the population in the North witnessed the implementation of the Welfare State in Norway. One consequence of this was a demographic change along the coast, caused by an out-migration of youths settling permanently in cities because of education or jobs. This led to a reduced recruitment to the traditional adaptions in the fiords and many of the outports were abandoned as the younger generation disappeared. These years also marked the beginning of some rather drastic ecological changes, namely the depletion of the capelin and cod stocks in the Barents Sea. Today, there does not seem to be much credibility left in the Norwegian fisheries management. The cod fisheries have collapsed, and what is left is strongly regulated through a system of quotas and licenses. The quotas follow the boat and are not transferable, which has led many to argue that a better solution would be to buy and sell the quotas in an open market.

Parallel to this development, *fish-farming* started up in northern Norway in the 1980s. Salmon and arctic char have been the most important species and a growing part of the production is being exported to an expanding market abroad. During the last couple of years, one has successfully been able to farm cod and there is now experimental farming going on with halibut. The appearance of this technology, knowledge and market, combined with national political support, led to a boom in the farming of fish. In political circles in Norway it is considered a solution to many of the economic problems of the rural population in the west and north of Norway. And quite a few have started to talk of fish-farming as *the* most important way to do fishing in the future.

The regulation of the fisheries in Norway then, is an example of ideological legitimation. The basic ideological view of Norwegian authorities has been the theory of the tragedy of the commons: if central authorities do not regulate access to fishing, then the inherent wish of the individual to maximize his own interests will in the long run inevitably empty the resources and thus threaten the common interests of all fishermen.

Looking upon the actual development in the fiords, however, we see that the problems of the fishing communities are actually consequences of this national political and legal view of the marine resources as common property, belonging to all Norwegian citizens. Because of this view, the marine tenure system of the local Sami population became rather invisible to Norwegian authorities. And if they were aware of this local practice in the fiords it was more or less regarded as an anacronism not to be reckoned with in a modern welfare state where equal rights for all citizens to any necessity were considered the cornerstone of society.

But the real paradox of it all, is the solution which Norwegian authorities are discussing when it comes to the problems which this traditional Sami tenure system has run into. That is *privatisation* of the fisheru resources. Today it is debated, whether management should be based upon a system of transferable quotas, that is quotas which can be bought and sold on an open market. Regarding fish-farming, the system is based upon the farmer's applying for exclusive rights in a part of the area in the fiord – normally not exceeding 1 km². A loan in the bank makes it possible to buy the necessary technology – which could be around 2-4 times his yearly income – and then he is in the position to start farming. So far, noone except a few local inhabitants, has started to ask questions about the legal implications of this partitioning and privatization of the sea. Fish-farming is regarded as such a promising economic enterprise that very few ask questions concerning its legal and practical consequences for traditional fishery management in the area.

The story of Sami marine tenure in the fiords of northern Norway then, is a story of conflicting management ideas. While the Sami regarded the fiordal resources as a *property in common* for the local population, the Norwegian authorities based their fisheries management upon the view of these resources as *common property*. Thus the implications of this policy were destruction of the very same resources, because access was considered open to everybody. Today, the same interest groups which caused a depletion of the capelin and cod stocks in the Barents Sea, are now arguing to make the resources *private property* as a solution to the problems created by the former policy of open access. This, however, is clearly in conflict with the more general ethno-political strategies of the Sami political organisations of Norway, and it could also be in conflict with the general international principles of human rights, which Norway has accepted. Whatever the outcome, there are turbulent times ahead in the Norwegian fisheries management.

References

H.S.Gordon 1954. "The economic theory of a Common Property Resource: the fishery." *Journal of Political Economy* 62:124-142.

G.Hardin1968. "The tragedy of the commons." *Science* 162:1243-1247.

O.Brox 1990. "The common property theory: epistemological status and analytical utility". *Human Organization* 3.

C.Smith 1990. *Samiske interesser og fiskeri- reguleringer.* Oslo: Utredning for Fiskeridept.

O.Brox 1984. *Nord-Norge: Fra almenning til koloni.* Bergen, Oslo, Tromsø: Universitetsforlaget.

Difference and Boundary in a Local Community

On the formation of local associations in West Greenland

Søren T. Thuesen

ABSTRACT

How do people in local communities in Greenland make use of associations for purposes *other* than the declared common object? and how do expressions of locality relate to those of ethnic and national identity in a colonial and post colonial setting? The article examines the relationship between the association as a form of organisation and expressions of difference and boundary on a number of different, but related levels: a national level, an ethnic level, a local level and an individual level. The author suggests that the Greenlandic local associations have had a great influence on social change, not by virtue of action, but by virtue of the highly ritualized practice of the associations.

Introduction: associations as symbolic expressions of community

There is more to life in a local community than a description of its economic and political institutions can possibly reveal. When we ask what local institutions and community *mean* to people living in a particular place, we are dealing with the *symbolic construction of community* and we are in the field of cultural studies. We are confronted with feelings and sentiments which people hold of their community. Such sentiments are often ambiguous and hard to give words and, therefore, tend to be expressed by means of symbols. A symbol is something that one holds in common with certain other people, but it is often very difficult to agree on the actual meaning of the symbol. Acknowledged symbols are subject to diverging interpretations by the individuals that hold them in common: 'The form of symbols may be common to those who bear the same culture, the meaning of the symbols, their contents, may differ' (Cohen 1987:13).

The British anthropologist Anthony P. Cohen has suggested the application of the notion of *belonging* as a main category when dealing with local identity or *locality* (Cohen 1982). *Community* is understood on the one hand as a group of people with something in common, e.g. the inhabitants of a certain place, but on the other hand as a relational conception – differences and similarities to other communities are counted in (Cohen 1985). The point is that the *boundary* of community is where ideas that discriminate the community from other places and groups are invested and expressed symbolically. Cohen places community along with e.g. justice, goodness and duty as areas which are so difficult to categorize that they are surrounded by the most ambiguous symbolisms (Cohen 1987).

I am referring to a number of excellent studies by Cohen, especially on the Shetlands, in which he examines the field of identity and community at different levels (also Cohen 1986). His interest is to study community, not from the outside or at the surface, but by attempting to penetrate the structure of community and looking 'outwards from its core' (Cohen 1985: 20). It is then a question of perspective: Cohen sees the local community, the wider society, the world, from a local point of view. Cohen's approach taking the perspective of remote communities (be it geographically or socially) and convincingly analysing how boundaries of a local community are symbolic constructions, has made me want to examine experiences of difference in Greenlandic local communities along these lines. So what I present here is a *preliminary* study of the symbolic construction of local boundaries in West Greenland.

Associations in Greenland

One way of looking at a local way of life is to investigate the more or less formally organised associations in a community. I speak of such organisations using the term *association* although I know that English often uses *club*. By *association* I mean formal and semi-formal organisations, including clubs. Associations are more than just organisations; they are means of communication and platforms for symbolic management of social differentiation and identity. In the history of the associations there are clues to the understanding of processes of identity management at the local level.

The 80th anniversary of the first Greenlandic association was celebrated in 1987. The Greenlandic associations of the beginning of this century are remembered with pride. In the first Greenlandic nationalist historiography they are regarded as an early step on the way towards Home Rule.[1] Thus the associations are placed in the order of national symbols along with the flag, the national anthem, the atlas and so forth.[2]

In spite of minor regional differences, the development of local associations proceeds correspondingly along the west coast of Greenland. The period from around 1910 to the '20s is dominated by the Christian and national revivalist movement and various associations derived from it. From the '20s a number of secular enlightenment associations and youth associations emerge. During the '30s the first sports associations come along, and within a few years in many towns also a competing – similar purpose – association. During the '40s and '50s interest groups such as fishermen's and women's associations as well as the first explicitly political associations are formed. After 1950 and the opening of Greenland various religious communities appear in Greenland establishing themselves as associations, just as a number of other Danish associations form local branches (e.g. scouts, Lions Club and trade unions).[3]

Today there is a multitude of associations in Greenland, both in settlements and in towns. Association activities are still a significant part of the way of life in a local community. The presence of associations is visible through the widespread use of symbols in the form of standards, logograms and badges and through the celebration of all kinds of jubilees. This emphatic, almost exaggerated marking of difference in space and time is a general feature of social life in Greenland today – in the ongoing process of nation building as well as in the parallel construction of local identity following the boundaries of the townships.

I shall be dealing with the activities of association in two local communities in West Greenland by the way of a number of cases and examples, some from before 1950, and some from recent years. The sources available and the literature on associations in Greenland are scanty. Hence, I shall rely partly on material which I collected during field work conducted in the Sisimiut (Holsteinsborg) and Maniitsoq (Sukkertoppen) areas over the years 1987-1989.[4]

Ritualized gathering: a one-year jubilee

For a start, I shall recount the one-year jubilee of an association that I attended in a West Greenlandic town in 1987. The association is called *Peqatigiinniat*

Inuusutaat (the Christian youth association) and is connected to the Greenlandic church. I was invited along with the local Greenlandic pastor. It was to the interest of the pastor to attend in order to show his support of community youth work in a town seriously lacking activities for young people. Similarly, it was obviously in the interest of the association to have the local head of the Church seated among them as a symbolic marking of the legitimacy of the association within the community.

We were on time, arriving at 6 p.m. to a small meeting house that is shared by the Young Peqatigiinniat and the Christian temperance society, Blue Cross. Well over 20 young people aged between 16 and 20 had turned up. The room was gaily decorated, with two long tables ready laid for dinner. At the end of these tables was placed yet another table which turned out to be the chairman's table. A three-branched candlestick and miniature staffs with the Danish and Greenlandic flag were placed at the middle of it. We sat down at the tables. The chairman bid everybody welcome, especially the pastor – I was introduced as a scientist studying the history of Peqatigiinniat. The chairman went through the programme of the evening and proposed a hymn for a start.

There was to be a general assembly before dinner. Apart from the election of the new committee there were two issues on the agenda: the choice of a standard and a badge for the association, and a proposal that the association should move a memorial which was now placed in an awkward spot, where access was difficult for aged members of the senior Peqatigiinniat. The election was conducted solemnly and correctly according to the statutes. Without much discussion, a committee almost identical to the one retiring was elected – consisting by the way exclusively of men. The last issue, moving the memorial, was passed as well without conflict. However, the choice of standard and badge, as it turned out, was to cause serious discussion, questioning of procedure and quite a number of ballots. It was not a question of whether or not they should have these standards and badges – that seemed to be a matter of course. And to my surprise, there was no discussion about whether to use the Greenlandic or Danish flag as a standard. To the young people of Peqatigiinniat it was obvious that a standard could only be *Dannebrog*, the Danish flag. The crucial problem was the text: what to write and with what kind of types? Several proposals were put forward, but after a while the vote was for a standard with the initials of the association and the year of foundation, *1987*, on the top corner in so-called *Gothic* typeface. I was astonished. Here I should say that Gothic has never been used for Greenlandic writing. In the 18th century, at the time when Gothic was used in Denmark, Roman types were employed in connection with Greenlandic written language (Gad 1985: 22).

My interpretation of these young people's choice of standard device is that they reveal a profound urge to place themselves in history. By placing the association in the year 1987, however recent it is, they seize a place in chronological history, and the future opens to a succession of jubilees like the one-year celebration. The use of Gothic letters constitutes the kind of exaggeration that lends a touch of patina and distinction to a perhaps too recent construction.

In this choice of symbols there is no indication of any need or wish to emphasize that this is a Greenlandic association. We should be cautious, nevertheless not to conceive of the choice of the Dannebrog as an indication that *the Greenlandic* is being renounced. Rather, I suggest that the refrainment from using the Greenlandic flag indicates a wish to avoid *Greenlandicness* in its specific Home Rule – nationalist – form. The Greenlandic flag does not arouse associations to age or history as is certainly the case with the Dannebrog. In fact, the Danish flag is still regarded as the Greenlandic flag proper by many Greenlanders and it is seen side by side with the new Greenlandic flag – just as was the case on the chairman's table (Kleivan 1988: 51).

After the general assembly we proceeded to a luxurious dinner – and, after yet another hymn, to an even more sumptuous orgy of sweets and sweet drinks. The young people were happy, chatting, and having a great time, and left in good order before midnight. I was puzzled by the fact that there was no discussion about Christianity or religious subjects at a general assembly and meeting of a Christian association – in fact the only indication of the Christian base was the hymns and the lack of alcohol. Evidently, this is not an association of action. Hence, it is a committee looking after its members in various ways. A good part of the members' subscriptions and any subsidies from the municipality is spent on social gatherings like this evening. The ritualized gathering, including the acting, out of forms prescribed in the statutes as well as the joint consumption of the resources of the association, is a general characteristic of Greenlandic associations.

The association as a form of organisation

As mentioned, the breakthrough in Greenland of the association as a particular form of organisation took place in the beginning of this century. The formation of a wide range of diverse associations can be seen as an expression of a commonly felt need for new forms of fellowship. Greenlandic society went through profound changes caused by the readjustment from sea mammal hunting to fishery, which meant a change-over to market economy and a gradual disintegration of the forms of fellowship related to the hunting culture (Thuesen 1988).

Basically, I see an association as a *formal organisation* defined by guidelines put down in statutes concerning the purpose of the association, criteria of membership, type and election of management and procedures of decision-making. Obviously, the Greenlandic associations link up with the tradition and practice of associations of Northern Europe and especially Denmark. This implies the use and recognition of a number of institutions tied to a specifically European perception of democracy, for instance the commitment to the status of written statutes and records and certain procedures concerning bodies of decision-making and election of representatives.

It is a remarkable feature of the type of organisation, with which we deal, that notwithstanding the different purposes of various associations, their structure and procedure are fundamentally the same. Associations are alike in the sense of having a purpose and way of functioning according to a set of rules stating the duties and rights of the members. However, the formation of an association calls for more than just statutes. Primarily, there must be a general consensus on what an association is about. Furthermore, certain skills in organising must be present within the group of founders. As it happens, there are at least a few individuals in most local communities who possess such organising abilities and who are called on when needed.[5]

In Greenlandic the words *peqatigiit* or *peqatigiiffik* are used for *association* – when translated the two words mean virtually the same, namely, *association* or *union*. The plural of *peqatigiit* indicates a plurality of individuals getting together, so an alternative translation could be *the united*.

Formal and semi-formal associations

However, in relation to the early associations, Greenlandic informants speaking of a particular association would sometimes claim that this association was no association *proper*. I asked a man about his membership of a youth association in the '30s. He answered that you could not become a member, but everybody who took an interest could participate. My comment to this was to suggest that when you could not become a member there would be no subscription either. 'No', he said, 'you didn't have to pay, but you would make a contribution.' This type of association was not unusual. The association had a name and a committee arranging enlightenment talks and public dances, but in a strict sense it was not a proper association. It was a small of group of people, more or less self-appointed, carrying out activities to the benefit of the community, but without involving people as formal members or decision-makers.

It appears from this example, that it is necessary to distinguish between at least two types of associations. I shall distinguish between *semi-formal associations*, like the one I have just described, and *formal associations* with statutes and membership proper.

Peqatigiinniat in Maniitsoq was the first association in Greenland. It was founded more than 80 years ago in 1907. The initiative was taken by a son of the local Greenlandic pastor. He himself was employed by the Royal Trade. Some years later, his brother, also a Trade employee, founded the so-called *Lecture Association* with the object of getting people together for enlightenment talks given by himself and other speakers.[6] This association is a *semi-formal association* unlike the *formal* Peqatigiinniat, which had statutes and subscription-paying members.

Common and exclusive associations

Looking at the local associations as they develop until recent years, it seems obvious that there is a call for a further typological distinction concerning the degree to which the associations structure the lives of their members. There must be a profound difference in meaning between being a member of a religious sect and of a sports club. I suggest we make a rough distinction between, on the one hand, *common associations* that provide the framework for pursuing certain goals (for instance trade unions and women's associations) or practicing certain activities like kayaking or singing and, on the other hand, *exclusive associations* which offer a fellowship or a way of life that exceeds the meetings and intervene profoundly within the lives of the members. There is often an element of revivalism or consciousness raising involved – be it religious or political. The notion of *ideological associations* could be used, but I prefer the notion of *exclusive associations* to emphasize the fact that membership of this kind of association excludes the possibility of simultaneous membership of competing associations. It is characteristic of the exclusive associations that they hold national or universal aims and, hence, are tied to national or international associations or organisations.

In recent years, many of the local common associations have united in national organisations, in my opinion to be able to influence national parliamentary and financing authorities.[7]

Nationality

It is difficult to make any clear distinction between national and ethnic identity in Greenland before 1950. In the beginning of the century early Greenlandic nationalism with its proud expressions of Greenlandic awareness in literature and songs was developing side-by-side with strategies to make Greenland a genuine and equal part of the Kingdom of Denmark. Nevertheless, the expressions of nationality of those days were of a different nature than the political and separatist nationalism of the '60s and '70s. When I eventually speak of nationality it is due to the fact that, already when Greenland was still formally a colony, there were tendencies towards Greenlanders recogniz-

ing their country and people as a nation. The formation of nation-wide associations played a role in making people think of Greenland as a national entity. Without getting into conceptual discussions of nationalism, I here suggest the use of the term *nationality* in the sense of 'feelings and awareness of a national entity'. Ethnicity then is 'feelings and awareness of cultural difference', that is, regardless of actual political realities.

Saved and non-saved

As an early example of exclusive associations which operated on a national scale, one could pick out Peqatigiinniat. This Christian and national movement was started with the acceptance of the Church of Greenland. It was not considered a sect, but rather an active supplement to the Church. Within a few years local associations were founded all along the west coast of Greenland. In 1917 these associations were united in a national organisation. The stimulus to the formation of these associations came partly from similar revivalist movements in Denmark. In Greenland there was in addition a remarkable focus on material questions and rather nationalist tendencies, especially during the early years.[8]

Peqatigiinniat were the first and for a period the only associations. The situation in the settlements therefore often tended to be one of two: either the whole population joined or for a while there would be a sort of balanced situation with the population divided pro et contra the association. However, even in these situations of division, it seems that opponents would turn up at the meetings to ask questions and criticize or simply for the entertainment and the variety which such a meeting brought to a small community (Thuesen 1988: 97f). Often, the element of revivalism in this association, that is the notion of being saved, would make the members regard themselves as fundamentally different and better than the non-saved. From time to time the result was demands for members' right to occupy the first row in church, etc. (Lynge 1981: 14).

Drinking and non-drinking

Like faith, drinking habits are of great significance to personal identity. The temperance associations can be seen to have grown out of the work of the Peqatigiinniat. As early as 1925 a local temperance association was formed in Maniitsoq (Sandgreen 1982: 139). During the '50s the number of temperance associations rose rapidly. The majority of these were affiliations of the international Christian *Blue Cross* organisation.[9]

I think of the Blue Cross associations as exclusive associations. Like Peqatigiinniat, they tend to produce a division of small communities into two groups: those who are in it, and those who are not. In an article on interpersonal relations in a small Greenlandic community Per Langgaard speaks of a *polarization* between drinkers and non-drinkers: 'A little less than half of the adult population of the village join or sympathize with the temperance movement, while the others drink heavily' (Langgaard 1985: 307).

Almost per definition, Blue Cross tends to create boundaries between members and non-members in a local community. Great effort is made to keep the members non-drinking, which often leads to a situation where members mainly socialize with each other. Furthermore, the generally more fortunate economic situation of non-drinkers may further the mutual social relations between non-drinkers and over time help bring about social climbing.

Siumut and Atassut

It would be interesting to compare the local organisational processes of Siumut and Atassut, the two new political parties during the '70s, to the organising of religious and temperance associations. The political party organisations are exclusive associations in the sense that you cannot be a member of both parties at the same time, but also because they have obviously tended to make everybody in small communities choose side. I would call them *complementary exclusive associations*. In an inspiring article *"New political structure and old non-fixed structural politics in Greenland"*, Jens Dahl puts forward the thesis that the introduction of a fixed dichotomic political structure on a national level causes a process of disintegration of the former flexible structure of alliances in small communities (Dahl 1985). Belonging to one of the two large political parties becomes crucial, as it affects every part of life in a community. Dahl gives an illustrative example of children of a settlement who play Atassut against Siumut on the football ground.

I suggest that it is possible that any small community tend to produce such dichotomic structures for the acting out of various social conflicts. Apparently both faith, drinking habits and politics tend to produce a remarkable *either/or*-difference in a local community; not in the sense that members of the community are divided into two fixed groups – since it seems quite easy for individuals to move to the other side of the boundary and back again, but in the sense of a structural either/or, i.e. a two-group division. Later, I intend to focus on the dichotomy of Danish/Greenlandic in Sisimiut in the '30s. As Jens Dahl shows, the ideological basis of both Siumut and Atassut in the '70s was determined by different stands towards Denmark, that is by different drawings of ethnic boundaries. In my opinion, the ethnic dichotomy is a structure that has proved useful throughout this century in relation to symbolic management of internal social inequality in Greenland.

Ethnicity

In the beginning of the century association members were almost exclusively Greenlandic, and only the Greenlandic language was used. When asked whether the associations were utilized for purposes of political or nationalist activity or discussion, several informants replied that of course this was not the object of the associations, but on the other hand... yes, of course, people talked about material matters and whatever happened in town. From this perspective, associations can be seen as not only formal arenas for carrying out certain activities like football or singing, but also as informal political arenas.

It seems as if Greenlandic criticism towards Danish authorities and towards the state of affairs was seldom put forward in public to a Danish audience but kept within the Greenlandic community. I am afraid there is no room here for a detailed elaboration of this point, but I see the Greenlandic debate of those days as a *restricted public sphere*, due to the Danish dominance and its local colonial representatives. In other words, the associations constitute a Greenlandic public sphere where Greenlanders were free to speak without interference from the Danes.

The Danish authorities were a bit anxious about the early Greenlandic attempts to organise. Recent experiences from other Danish colonies gave rise to fears of getting an 'Icelandic or West Indian situation' in Greenland.[10] One of my informants stressed the fact that before 1950 there was no liberty of association in Greenland. If you wanted to found an association, you had to ask for a permission from the local Danish manager of the Trade or from the pastor. To my knowledge, there was no law against organising, but there is no doubt about the fact that the wish of the manager was command to the community. Actually, some of the managers behaved like small kings.

Sujumut/Frem in Sisimiut

I shall point out the activities of a single person who was a founder of associations in Sisimiut and Copenhagen in the '30s. His name is Carl Broberg. He was a radical of his time and a controversial character in the eyes of Danes and many Greenlanders. His work is a fine illustration of the element of friction along the Danish/Greenlandic boundary that was part of the experience of the early associations.

Carl Broberg and his wife Else told me that they settled in Sisimiut in 1931. He was appointed manager of the local ship-yard and she was a nurse, although not employed as such in Sisimiut. He came from north Greenland and she was Danish. The fact that Broberg, a Greenlander, had been trained in Denmark and was now a person in charge and, in addition to this, was married to a Danish woman, put him in a very delicate position vis-à-vis the local Danish authorities. It caused daily disputes and conflicts of competence between him and the Danish manager of the Trade. Another result was that the Broberg couple, being a mixed couple, was to some extent excluded from the closed Danish group of Sisimiut. At the time, there was no socializing whatsoever between the two ethnic groups, so they told me.

Broberg knew how to start an association. In Denmark he had been a member of a rowing club – that was where he got his organising experience. Together with a couple of other Greenlanders, also trained in Denmark, they got together in Sisimiut in 1932 and founded an association aimed at initiating activities mainly for the youth of the town. They agreed that the association should be 'unpolitical and to the benefit of the community'. The activities were skiing, dog sledge racing, talks on enlightenment and progress, keeping the town nice and clean and social gatherings with coffee. The activities were financed by monthly subscriptions from the members.

At the founding meeting there was a major discussion concerning the name of the association. Broberg wanted to call it *Sujumut* (forward), while others, the majority, thought that *Frem* (forward in Danish) would be better. The discussion was not over the meaning of the name, but whether to use the Danish or the Greenlandic word. I see the proposal of the Danish name, which was eventually passed, as an indication of the need to make the association *intelligible* and acceptable to the Danes. By using a Danish name, the association was made "proper". Hence, it was not just a Greenlandic association, it was more like the Danish associations.[11]

Peqatigît Kalâtdlit in Copenhagen

The Broberg couple left Sisimiut and Greenland in 1936, objecting to the 'system' and the discrimination he had experienced. In Copenhagen he continued his activities on another level, namely, as the co-founder of the association *Peqatigît Kalâtdlit* (The Association of Greenlanders) in 1939. There were several incidents of conflict between this association and the Greenland Board, that is the colonial department, but, operating in Denmark, the association was able to refer to the liberty of association and, hence, avoid attempts of interference and control.[12] A very important task of the association was the publishing of a magazine, called *Kalâtdlit*, which was sent to Greenland in great numbers for distribution in most of the towns. Letters from readers show that the magazine was received with gratitude and great expectations. Pavia Petersen writes from Maniitsoq:

> "Being in the beautiful Greenland, – having such difficulty getting together for association activities due to our scattered habitations and because of the huge stretch of our land, badly regretting the lack of a members' magazine to unite us – we hope that our brothers and sisters in

Denmark shall not forget us in their doings. ... We thank you very much for the members' magazine which was sent to us for distribution." (Kalâtdlit, no. 3 1939: 3f – my translation).

In 1940 Peqatigît Kalâtdlit urges Greenlanders in Greenland to become members, and the idea of a nation-wide national organisation is now obvious (Kalâtdlit, no. 1 1940). From Qaqortoq Rink Kleist writes:

> "During recent years, it has become more and more evident how important it is that Greenlanders who have been in Denmark, and those who are presently there, have a positive influence and capability of performing in our country. Therefore, I ask you, my fellow countrymen, who are presently in Denmark and who have formed an association for the sake of our country and our nationality, always to remember what your country and your people expect from you.' (Kalâtdlit, no. 2 1940: 1 – my translation).

Producing the magazine, the association provided Greenlanders with a forum for national and controversial issues and hereby supported the activities of many local associations.

Locality

I would like to take a closer look at the associations and communities of Sisimiut and Maniitsoq. I am focusing on *local identity*, although I realize that it is impossible to produce a coherent or unambiguous description of a specific identity. We are able to distinguish differences in what people say and think of themselves in two different communities, but such statements can only be seen as aspects of a local identity. Referring to A. P. Cohen, local identity, or as he puts it 'the reality of community in people's experience', is constructed through the continuous attachment of community members to a common body of symbols. The very different individuals belonging to a community are involved in the process of boundary-maintaining, that is to say producing, maintaining and further developing the commonality of symbol (Cohen 1985:16). The term *identity* implies similarity and being alike, but has to do with difference and boundary, whether we speak of personal, collective, social, local, ethnic, cultural or national identity. Processes of identity construction are expressed through the symbolic drawing of boundaries.

The communities: Maniitsoq and Sisimiut

Turning to the communities in question, I shall now give a very brief introduction. In the beginning of the century Maniitsoq was the largest town in Greenland with about 600 inhabitants. This town had a number of different associations. Sisimiut, the neighbouring town to the north, had only a few hundred inhabitants and just 5 or 6 associations altogether up until 1950. Today, Sisimiut has grown larger than Maniitsoq with just over 5.000 inhabitants compared to the about 4.000 of Maniitsoq. Sisimiut is an expanding town. Coming from the outside, one experiences a strong sense of enterprise and dynamism. If not – people will tell you that these are characteristics of their community. Maniitsoq in comparison, is quiet. The town was not favoured in the post-war development planning in Greenland. Public transportation between Maniitsoq and other places is rather infrequent, which leaves the impression of an isolated town. However, during recent years, quite a number of prestige buildings and projects have been initiated by local authorities in an almost symbolic attempt to wipe out the image of stagnation. People of Maniitsoq speak of the achievements of their local associations of the past as something special and unique. Local history is mobilized in the efforts to produce symbols of identity. The glorious past is now a characteristic of Maniitsoq.

In Sisimiut, I looked for local views on the reason why there were only a few associations in this town in the beginning of the century. In his explanation, one informant made a connection between a specific local characteristic and associations as democratic fora. I quote:

> "For a start, it must be clear that there was no democracy in the old society. Those who would not work and contribute to the community had to die. Very often, young people of today don't realize this. *Forstanderskaberne* (the first parliamentary councils of Greenland) were meant to teach people rules of democracy, but, as they were primarily concerned with economic distribution, it turned out to mean the right of superior force, that is to say the right of the superior hunters. In this town, you experience individualism to a degree you wouldn't dream of, as well as rejection of cooperation. People recognize the principles of democracy as long as it doesn't affect their personal economic income.'

It is interesting that individualism and considerations of personal status and economy is seen as local characteristics of Sisimiut today. Carl and Else Broberg claimed that in the '30s certain parts of the Greenlandic community were not inclined to join or support the association. I quote Else Broberg:

> "Greenlanders holding a position, being employed at a slightly higher level than other Greenlanders, did actually not have the courage to support. Although they probably agreed with the association in their hearts, they were afraid of getting involved. They couldn't just get another job, so they had to keep their mouths shut. And that was what they were paid for, you see."

Difference

I mentioned in the beginning that I have noticed that local associations tend to exaggerate the marking of difference through symbols, and this to a degree where the object of the association seems less important. In 1945 a Danish observer complains about the Greenlandic youth and sports associations: 'The case is that it is 'something' to be a member of an associa-

tion and to have a special shirt. The rest, the object, the essential, is of no interest' (Winding 1945: 49). Following this statement, I suggest that access to prestige may be what makes associations so attractive.

In the modern communities of Sisimiut and Maniitsoq a number of positions of power and prestige are offered in relation to municipal structures. Within the parliamentary system there is a hierarchy of boards, committees and sub-committees, each with a chairman. As a supplement to this structure, there exists another set of prestige positions within the committees of the local associations. In principle, it is easy to move in and out of various association committees and positions. As mentioned earlier, the structure and procedure of associations are fundamentally the same, notwithstanding their different objects. Some people choose, as a strategy, to participate in various association activities as a parliamentary learning process in order to qualify for future engagement in politics.[13]

However, the struggle for the positions offered reflects more than just topical conflicts and interests. Apparently, there is often long standing competition or conflicts between families or groups of families. Certain prominent families seem to be in charge of specific associations. One informant told of demands from one particular family on special services from a public institution. For several years, this family had held positions of chairman and committee of an association which in its object relates specifically to the institution in question. Family dominance of an association is often hard to recognize because of the possibility of indirectly exerting control through distant or affinal relatives. However, dominance is not necessarily intended or part of some consciously held strategy.

During recent years a great number of people have moved to the towns from surrounding settlements. It has created a situation of struggle for political influence. This goes not only for positions in local councils, but also for positions with a certain symbolic glow to it, as is the case of some association chairman positions. It will certainly be noticed if a first generation newcomer is elected mayor. And, if you have not got the luck to be elected for the Council, it might be of some comfort at least to be able to sign yourself as chairman of some association. This could be an explanation of the fact that, in some places, there is quite a number of 'empty' or 'sleeping' associations. By 'sleeping' associations I mean associations without any activities or meetings and with hardly any members, but still existing by virtue of the board and a chairman.

In a study of the associations of Sisimiut in the beginning of the '70s, Birte Haagen finds that newcomers are especially attracted to the associations (Haagen Petersen 1972).[14] Associations are in principle democratic organisations, open to everybody, and newcomers without social relations in town may have the choice of joining an association as a means or a springboard to other social networks and potential future influence.

Conflict and silence

It is my impression that conflicts between Greenlandic families are rarely spoken of and especially not to strangers – Danes in particular. Intra- as well os inter-family conflicts are surrounded with silence and modesty and the solving of conflicts is left to the conflicting parties.[15] Only when a conflict holds clearly ludicrous elements people will talk of it and, especially, laugh about it, while still making sure that those involved are not confronted with the comments. *Social inequality*, which obviously exists, is another issue that is surrounded with silence. Explanations of inequality as difference of class and family are strongly rejected as a 'Danish' way of seeing things. To outsiders, Danes in particular, an image of common Greenlandic interests and solidarity within the local community is maintained.

Cohen distinguishes between *pragmatic* and *rhetorical* expressions of egalitarianism, regarding circumstances where people find it appropriate to act as though they were equal (Cohen 1985). Pragmatic egalitarianism will be the case, for instance, in small or isolated communities or groups where members seek to avoid conflict, because there is no way of escaping. However, when egalitarianism is expressed across the boundary of a local community, it also becomes a rhetorical expression of the integrity of community:

> "It is the presentation to the outside world of the common interests of the members of the community. As such, it bears the characteristic hallmark of communication between different levels of society; namely, simplification. When a group of people engages with some other, it has to simplify its message down to a form and generality with which each of the members can identify their personal interests. Otherwise the message becomes impossible convoluted and so heavily qualifies as to be unintelligible to the outsider. ... Further, the expression of egalitarianism across the boundary may often also be a means by which the community expresses its difference from those elsewhere. Its members may denigrate the disparities of wealth and power, or the competitiveness which they perceive elsewhere, to justify and give value to their espousal of equality." (Cohen 1985: 35).

In my understanding, Cohen explains the outward expressions of egalitarianism as a question of a simplified, intelligible communication of *community* by virtue of a 'lowest common denominator'. I do not find the explanation fully satisfactory when it comes to the Greenlandic *under-communication* of inequality to outsiders. I would rather suggest that the simplification, the assertion of egalitarianism, may *exactly* be aimed at veiling conflicts in order to protect community from possible criticism and interference by others – an interference that people themselves are abstaining from. And I would say that the Danes in particular have

been known for their perpetual criticism and interference with Greenlandic affairs. Hence, there is an interest in offering Danes a picture of Greenlandic society which contrasts Danish society as better, more equal and without mutual competition.

I must admit that the silence surrounding social conflicts makes it difficult to draw conclusions on how social difference is symbolised on a local level. I suggest that there is a coherence between silence on conflicts and people's urge to be surrounded with symbols of difference.

Individuality

When we speak of associations in relation to identity, we must not forget that we are dealing with people, individuals, who make choices. In relation to some associations, members make personal choices of extensive social consequence. I am referring to the neo-religious movements. During recent years *identity* has been a general topic of debate in Greenland. Not just national identity and the identity as a Greenlander, but also *personal identity,* including life-perspectives and future possibilities, has been of concern. Looking for explanations of the large number of suicides, e.g., there has been attempts to understand this in terms of 'identity conflicts'. I am not very fond of such explanations, but it is yet another indication that the category of the individual is crucial.

Jehovah's Witnesses

To my surprise, from what I have seen and heard of, it seems that currently, neo-religious movements such as *Jehovah's Witnesses* are gaining ground in Greenland. In Nuuk there are quite a number of different sects and religious communities. These years some of them experience a growing number of Greenlandic members. For these observations I rely on information from friends and acquaintances in Nuuk who are quite familiar with these movements. I am aware that the actual number of new members of such organisations may not be so impressive[16], but what is important is that people in Nuuk notice that something unusual is going on. It is a subject of discussion and concern to many people.

When Inge Kleivan in 1979 described the religious sects in Greenland, she did not foresee any future growth of such organisations. I quote:

> "Nobody seems to expect the emergence of a religious revival in Greenland, neither within nor outside the Church, which can see people through the problems that characterize life these years. However, many people seem to rely on the fact that the rising political consciousness in connection with future Home Rule may create a more harmonious Greenlandic society." (Kleivan 1979: 141).

Apparently, the political revival of the '70s and '80s may be about to be replaced by a religious revivalism of a new generation.

Jehovah's Witnesses have been in Greenland since the '50s. The organisation has affiliations in all major towns and, for many years, it has published its magazine *The Watchtower* in Greenlandic.

The movement offers an all-embracing fellowship as well as activities to such an extent that it takes up all spare time of the members: activities such as biblical studies, rhetorical training and door-to-door calls. A life according to certain rules of conduct is expected from the members. Membership, therefore, means that actual social and family relations may be endangered or even cut off. One of the rules are concerned with blood. The rule not to consume blood and have blood transfusions is hard to accept for many Greenlanders. However, this does not mean that Jehovah's Witnesses give up e.g. reindeer hunting; it is merely a matter of draining the blood of the animal immediately upon killing it.

The motivation for becoming a Jehovah's Witness is explained by the members in a religious discourse, namely, as a question of personal experience of revival. Quite often, the kind of life people turn away from has been one characterized by alcohol abuse and personal and family conflicts. Thus, it is tempting to suggest that, behind the explicit motivations, the religious community and its rules may as well be thought of as a means of avoiding actual social and family ties.

Jehovah's Witnesses is an international organisation. It promotes thinking among its members in terms of a global community and does not believe in human power, neither within individual relationships nor within human institutions, be it the Church or parliamentary political institutions. In practice, this means that Jehovah's Witnesses seek to refrain from exercising power, partly by seeking employment without superior functions, partly by not mingling in politics. They only acknowledge God and His power; therefore, they do not respect the Church of Greenland, political parties, Home Rule or Greenlandic nationalism.

It seems to me that certain other motives for membership appear, namely, a reaction and resistance to the demands of social involvement during the last ten years of Home Rule as well as the never ending discussions of Greenlandic identity. Becoming a Jehovah's Witness is a personal choice of a peaceful, harmonious and industrious (family) life and, at the same time, it implies a renunciation of a chaotic, conflict-laden social reality. A woman in Nuuk, who was not a member, mentioned that the reason why she liked them was that they were always happy, open-minded and eager to talk, unlike most other people: 'And they have such nice, harmonious families and lovely children.' It seems to me that these virtues correspond to virtues attributed *good old days* in Greenland.

The growth of Jehovah's Witnesses and other neo-religious movements is probably mainly a phenomenon of the towns, but it is part of a general tendency towards individualisation which is most clearly expressed in the *big town* Nuuk. The movements are just one, but striking, example of associations promoting the *individual* and ideas of an open choice of 'cultural' orientation. One could mention, as another example, the growing popularity of e.g. Asian fighting sports, like karate and tae kwon do, and other sports where individual performance and feat is essential, such as skiing and marathon race. Frequently, Greenlandic sportsmen participate in international games and world championships. In 1989 for the first time, Greenland won a world championship – in tae kwon do. The most successful sportsmen are celebrated in the media as national 'heros' and appointed 'Sportsman of the Year' – some of them are made to figure in advertisements for sweet drinks, etc. The media in Greenland are offering plenty of such images of individual achievement and of the possibility of individual orientation in directions elsewhere in the world. In this sense, individuality, nationality and the various other identity categories in Greenland are presently being expressed within the framework of an overall, worldwide sense of *internationality*.[17]

Conclusion

In recent years, Greenland has experienced a powerful nation building process which has been reflected among other things in an intense activity as regards construction and introduction of national symbols. Greenland has got Home Rule, its own flag, its own College of Heralds and almost all other symbols of modern nation states. As part of the same process, a local production of symbols has taken place at municipal and community level. Municipal coats of arms and local histories have been established, and certain characteristics have been chosen to figure as logograms and badges. This way of marking difference however, is only the temporary culmination of a process which has been going on in the local communities since the associations were introduced in the beginning of the century.

Besides the actual activities taking place in the local associations, these have played an important part as fora of public debate; as bases of political participation, as prestigious starting points, and, finally, as media of symbolic acting-out of social conflicts as well as possibilities of realization of individual life strategies.

To summarize the argument of this article, it does make sense to speak of the Greenlandic associations' thorough impact on social change – not by virtue of action, but by virtue of the highly ritualized practice of the associations. As regards the discussion concerning expression and assertion of difference in a local community, I would like to add one final remark. Cohen emphasizes again and again the *variability of meaning* of common symbols and states that 'in the face of this variability of meaning the consciousness of community has to be kept alive by manipulation of its symbols' (Cohen 1987:16). It is behind this perhaps vague notion of 'manipulation', that we find all the 'silent' social fussing and fighting for who is to define and decide. The task for us, then, is to examine the nature of this manipulation – the *process* of boundary-maintenance. It is not easy, but it is in this struggle for the right to define community that we may learn of the way internal social differences are linked with differences and definitions at national and supranational levels. In other words, the symbolic construction of community is a reflection of linkages between local struggles concerning social inequality and external integrating forces of nationality and internationality.

Notes

1. Petersen, H. C. 1987.
2. Inge Kleivan has done a study on the creation of the new Greenlandic flag, which is one of the chief national symbols (Kleivan 1988). Recently, Robert Petersen has dealt with the issue of contemporary Greenlandic identity and the construction of national symbols (Petersen 1990). In fact, he does not use the term *national identity*. He speaks instead of a new *structural identity* or structurally based identity as a supplement to Greenlandic ethnic identity. He refers to Greenland as an increasingly *bi-ethnic* society where Greenlanders as well as resident Danes – Danish Greenlanders – tend to regard Greenland as a national unit distinct from Denmark.
3. I regard the early women's associations as interest organisations, although they were platforms of ideological or political aims as well. Frequently, religious sects tend to use loose movement-like ways of organising, but basically their type of organisation is that of the association including the recognition of statutes, membership, subscription and so on. The Scouts' associations were established in Greenland in the '50s, but in Nuuk a Group of scouts a Y.M.C.A. type was started by Sofus Olsen as early as the '30s (according to information from Jørgen Petersen, Sisimiut). In 1943 Klaus Møller started a proper *Y.M.C.A. Scouts Group* in Nuuk (cf. Binzer et al 1957: 234).
4. The periods of field research were part of a larger research project concerning the Greenlandic catechist institution 1850-1950, financed by the Danish Research Council for the Humanities. The results will be presented in full in 1991.
5. Cf. Cohen, 1987: 28. In relation to the early Greenlandic associations, it seems evident that especially the college-trained catechists are the ones that take on the positions as organisers or association builders and consider the associations as instruments in their efforts to bring about 'enlightenment and civilization' to their communities. To the catechists, the new platforms provided by the associations, were of great importance in their promoting themselves as cultural élite and social class (cf. Thuesen 1990).
6. For a brief presentation of the early associations of Maniitsoq, see Møller 1982.
7. Whether speaking of one type of association or the other, nation-wide organisations are of course of important as symbolic accounts of sentiments of national solidarity or nationhood (cf. Petersen, R. 1990: 8).
8. I have done a detailed study of the early development of Peqatigiinniat from the start in 1907/08 to the union in 1917 (Thuesen 1988).
9. In 1956 there were 46 active Blue Cross associations holding about 1200 members (cf. Granum-Jensen 1979).
10. See for instance Knud Balle's review of the first Greenlandic novel in 1917. He warns against nationalism, fanaticism and socialism and foresees that without enlightenment and reforms in Greenland there will, within a few years, be at issue a 'Greenlandic question in the same sense as there has long been an Icelandic and a West Indian one' (Balle 1917).
11. During the first years, *Frem* had about 50 paying members. There were many female members, but none of these were members of the board. In 1950 the association (now under the name *Sujumut*) got together with two other sport associations *Amerdloq* and *Kunuk* and formed the association *S.A.K.* which still exists as a sport association. The name S.A.K. consists of the initials of the former associations.
12. Already at the founding general assembly (April 15, 1939) there was a discussion of the relationship to the Greenland Board and of the need to get the Board's permission to form the association: 'It was proposed to ask permission from the Board in advance, but this proposal was later rejected as we agreed that it was not necessary, because we, Greenlanders, staying in this country, are subject to Danish law.' (Kalâtdlit, no. 1: 3). Einar Lund Jensen characterizes Peqatigiit Kalaallit as a *'hjemstavnsforening'*, which in translation would be something like, 'association of expatriates', (literally home association), but he adds – referring to Carl Broberg – that the organising activities itself caused 'a certain scepticism or resistance' from the Danish authorities (Lund Jensen 1989: 286).
13. E. g. Manuel and Posluns relates of individual organising strategies involving association activities, in this case among Canadian indians (Manuel & Posluns 1978: 117).
14. The survey of Birte Haagen presents a very interesting material on associations and association members of Sisimiut. The focus is on associations as a means of interaction, as a means of levelling mutual difference and as a means of gaining influence. The survey of 1971/72 confirms my own opinion that, generally, there is a high representation of certain skilled individuals in the positions of the association boards, but unfortunately, the survey does not contribute data on family backgrounds or family network. Birte Haagen deals with the participation – and influence – of Danes in local associations, a question I have to leave out in this article.
15. This applies as well to conflicts of a more violent nature like e.g. wife-beating (cf. Sørensen 1990). Bo Wagner Sørensen has applied 'silence' as an analytic concept on Greenlandic material (Sørensen 1991).
16. According to information obtained in november 1990 from Jehovah's Witnesses in Denmark, there are a few hundred members in Greenland. The expansion within the last couple of years in Nuuk is said to amount to about 40 people, mainly young Greenlandic couples. This figure regards the number of new *baptized* members. There might be a substantial number of people who still have not joined, but can be considered a periphery to the organisation. I have not got information on the number of members of other neo-religious organisations in Nuuk.
17. In a critical comment on nationalism Jonathan Rée has suggested a rehabilitation of the notion of *internationality*: 'By internationality I do not mean what is usually meant by internationalism: a willingness to overlook national interest in favour of the welfare of humanity as a whole. Internationality is a style of thought and global organisation which tries to generate a plurality of nations, in order that, for any piece of land, and for any human being, there should be a definite answer to the question "which nation is responsible?" Internationality, you might say, is the tendency for the global imposition of the nation-form' (Rée 1991).

References

Balle, Knud. 1917 "I anledning af En Grønlænders Drøm". In: *Meddelelser fra den grønlandske Kirkesag, nr. 35. København.*

Binzer, K. et al: 1957 (eds.). *ilíniarfigssuaq. Godthåb seminarium. 1907-1957.*

Cohen, Anthony P. 1982: *Belonging. Identity and social organisation in British rural cultures.* Manchester University Press.
1985. *The Symbolic Construction of Community.* London: Routledge.

1986. *Symbolising Boundaries. Identity and diversity in British cultures.* Manchester University Press.

1987. *Whalsay. Symbol, segment and boundary in a Shetland island community.* Manchester University Press.

Dahl, Jens 1985. "New political structure and old non-fixed structural politics in Greenland". In Jens Brøsted et al. Eds.: *Native Power. The quest for autonomy and nationhood of indigenious peoples.* Oslo: Universitetsforlaget.

Gad, Finn 1985. "Læse- og skrivekyndigheden i 1700- og 1800-tallet indtil 1880." *GRØNLAND.* In Vagn Skovgaard-Petersen, Ed.: *Da menigmand i Norden lærte at skrive* – en sektionsrapport fra 19. nordiske historikerkongres 1984. København: Danmarks Lærerhøjskole.

Granum-Jensen, A. R. 1979(?). *Blå Kors' historie i 100 år.* Haderslev.

Haagen Petersen, Birte 1972(?). *Foreningsliv i Grønland.* Stencilat. København: Institut for Eskimologi.

Jakobsen, John 1990. *Timersorneq. Sport '90.* Nuuk: Atuagassiivik/ Eskimo Press.

Kalâtdlit 1939f (Magazine of the Greenlander Association in Denmark). Peqatigît Kalâtdlit. København.

Kleivan, Inge 1988. "The creation of Greenland's new national symbol: the flag". FOLK vol.30. Copenhagen.

1979: "Sprog og kirke i Grønland". In Bjarne Basse & Kirsten Jensen, Eds.: *Eskimosprogenes vilkår i dag.* Århus.

Langgaard, Per 1985. "Modernization and traditional interpersonal relations in a small Greenlandic community: A case study from Southern Greenland". *Arctic Anthropology* 23 (1 & 2).

Lund Jensen, Einar 1989. "Peqatigît Kalâtdlit – Grønlænderforeningens første år". *Tidsskriftet Grønland, nr. 9.*

Lynge, Hans 1981. *Grønlands indre liv. Erindringer.* Nuuk.

Manuel, George & Michael Posluns 1978. "Den fjerde verden. En indiansk virkelighed". København: Informationsdag.

Møller, Karl 1982. "Skolen og kulturelt arbejde". In: *Manîtsoq-Sukkertoppen 1782-1982.* Manîtsup kommunia.

Petersen, H. C. (ed.) 1987. *"Kalaallit oqaluttuarisaanerat. 1925-p tungaanut".* Nuuk.

Petersen, Robert 1990. "On the development of the Greenlandic identity". Paper from 7th Inuit Studies Conference, August 19 – 31, 1990. Fairbanks, Alaska.

Rée, Jonathan 1991. "Internationality". *Arbejdspapir,* no. 80. Center for Kulturforskning. Århus.

Sandgreen, Otto 1982. *Menigheden.* In: *Manîtsoq-Sukkertoppen 1782-1982.* Manîtsup kommunia.

Sørensen, Bo Wagner 1990. "Folk Models of Wife-Beating in Nuuk, Greenland". *FOLK* vol. 32. Copenhagen.

1991. "Sigende tavshed: køn og etnicitet i Nuuk, Grønland". *Tidsskriftet Antropologi* København.

Thuesen, Søren T. 1988. *Fremad, opad! Kampen for en moderne grønlandsk identitet.* København: Rhodos.

1990: "På vejen mod selvstændighed". *Tidsskriftet HUMANIORA,* no. 1. København.

Winding, Ole 1945. *"Grønland 1945".* København.

Class Interests and Nationalism in Faroese Politics

Jógvan Mørkøre

ABSTRACT

Party politics in the Faroe Islands is usually described by the right/left – and unionism/nationalism-dichotomies, either seeing them as separate and exclusive dimensions or postulating that nationalism is a rightist phenomenon. The history of the Faroese party system indicates that it is not a fixed matter which classes are to become nationalist – or *unionist* (i.e. *for* the union with Denmark) – and that the political dispute as to the union with Denmark has always been basically economic. There seems to be a correlation between the set-up of the political party system and the specific way that money from the Danish state subsidies are flowing into the islands.[1]

Introduction

What is more important in Faroese politics – the conflict between right and left or the conflict between unionism and nationalism. This controversy, which never seems to find an end, will be the issue of this article. I will try to form a general view of some questions that I think are relevant and important to investigate, if we shall ever be able to grasp nationalism in Faroese politics.

Usually Faroese politics is characterised by two dichotomies.[2] On the one hand the dichotomy between left and right, or we could say socialism and liberalism. On the other hand we have the dichotomy concerning the relations to the factual political union with Denmark (Home Rule 1948), between unionism and nationalism, or we could say confederalism and separatism.

This way of differentiation in portraying Faroese politics is often considered special. The dichotomy between left and right is one widely known. But the other one, the dichotomy between unionism and nationalism, is often perceived as being something especially Faroese. The reason why the Faroese see their politics as being either abnormal or something unique is obviously because we compare our politics to politics in the Nordic countries, but only to those that are sovereign states. Obviously this is a big mistake. Firstly, because the Nordic party systems are particularly *homogeneous* in the sense that they are firmly linked to class conflicts compared to many other countries in the world, where criteria such as language, religion, region, or nationality provide party systems with the basis for other kinds of dichotomies.[3] Secondly, because party systems in semi-autonomous areas obviously have to be considered on their own terms.[4]

Nevertheless, in the following, I am going to make a comparison with the Nordic party system both to locate similarities and – in particular – to point out dissimilarities. That will be done in a *dynamic* perspective. The development of the Faroese party system and its changeable characteristics will be described. The comparison will be made between the party systems as they were shortly before World War II. The aim is to situate the nationalist upheavals, identify the actors on the political scene behaving in the most nationalist – and unionist – way and hence have a short glance at their relationship to organisations and groupings on the labour market.

The considerations will be very *schematic*, which opens to a – perhaps unfortunate – degree of *determinism*, i.e. economic determinism and class determinism. For now it will be left to future research to outline complementing schemes of analysis to make the view less simplified.

The political parties

The names in Faroese are to the left, in the centre are the main ideological features, and in the column to the right the years of foundation.

In the middle column some of the ideological features are emphasised and some are placed in brackets. The emphasis indicates the main political doctrine, the brackets that this ideological feature is subordinated to the former.

In the following I shall not use the Faroese party names without calling them by their main characteristic and then stick to these characteristics, assuming that this will make it easier to associate with similar parties in neighbouring countries.

Sambandsflokkurin	*Unionists* (liberals)	1906
Sjálvstýrisflokkurin	*Autonomists* (social liberals)	1909
Javnaðarflokkurin	*Social Democrats* (unionists)	1925
Vinnuflokkurin Fólkaflokkurin	*Conservatives* (federalists)	1935/ 1939
Tjóðveldisflokkurin	*Separatists* (populists)	1948
Kristiligi Fólkaflokkurin	*Christians* (populists)	1955*
Sosialistiski Loysingarflokkurin	*Socialist separatists*	1990**

(*) The party was not originally a Christian party but became so in the eighties.
(**) Not represented in the Løgting but running for election November 1990.

Fig. 1. The political parties

The Unionist Party – Sambandsflokkurin – was founded in 1906. After the foundation they claimed themselves to be liberals. *The Autonomists*[5] – Sjálvstýrisflokkurin – organised themselves as a reaction to the formation of the Unionists. The year 1909 marks the year when their first party programme was published. Then there was a break.

In the years of world recession left-wingers and right-wingers formed new parties. The *Social Democratic Party* – Javnaðarflokkurin – came into being in 1925. It was also from the very beginning a unionist party. The *Conservative Party* was founded 10 years later as a reaction against the Keynesian way of budgeting the public expenditures, which the Social Democrats pushed forward. In addition the Conservatives was a federalist party, especially after merging with a former charismatic Autonomist leader, Jóannes Patursson, leaving his old party. After the merging the party in 1939 changed its name to Fólkaflokkurin.[6]

Although the Conservatives were a more radical party than the autonomists in questions regarding autonomy, no thorough separatist party was represented in the local parliament, the *Løgting,* until 1948. This new party named itself Tjóðveldisflokkurin. Here we will call it the *Separatists.*[7]

In addition to the four big parties in Faroese politics, the Unionists, the Social Democrats, the Conservatives, and the Separatists, and in addition to the former big party, the Autonomists, which nowadays is a small party, the *Christians*[8] should be mentioned. It is a small party, which has been changing its programme and ideological orientation several times. It was not originally a Christian party – not until the eighties, although it was founded back in 1955.

The last party on the list is a new left wing socialist or communist party[9] running for the first time for election to the Løgting, November 1990. Socialist planning and total independence from Denmark are the main features in their political programme.

Now let us fix the parties represented in the Parliament today in a diagramme generated on the two dichotomies mentioned earlier, left and right, and unionism and seperatism.

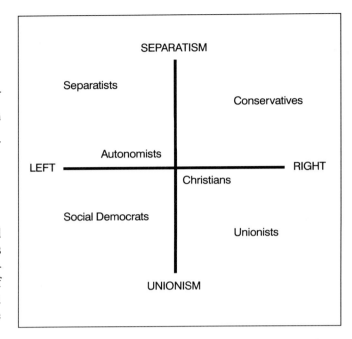

Fig. 2. The system of political parties – until recently

This figure is very commonly used to describe Faroese politics – and widely accepted. There has occasionally been some disagreement, as to whether the Social Democrats should be placed to the left or to the rigth of the Separatists,[10] but in general there is a consensus that the four big parties are placed in the corners of each their political room. The Social Democrats have the leftist/unionist room, the Unionists have the rightist/unionist room, the Conservatives have a rightist/separatist room and the political room, possessed by the Separatists is the leftist/separatist room. The smaller parties are located where the dichotomies are crossing each other.

This makes up a picture of the party system that is illustrative and easy to grasp. At the same time this presents a picture which has been almost unchanged from the mid-fifties and until recently. Today it seems that the bigger parties are leaving the corners in their political rooms and approaching the axes. This *political rotation* in the system of political doctrines goes with the sun, as described in Fig. 3. *(See page 59).*

This allegation is based on the parties' rhetoric and propaganda when they were running for elections to the Danish Parliament, *the Folketing,*[11] in 1987 and in 1988. First we had the Social Democrats and the Conservatives beating each other. The Social Democrats claimed the main threath to be economic liberalism. And vice versa: the Conservatives warned against the socialist enemy. In spite of this harsh polarisation

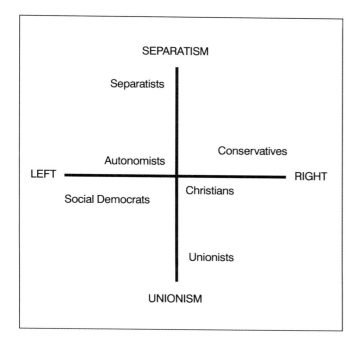

Fig. 3. The system of political parties – current tendencies

along the dichotomy left and right, there was a certain degree of agreement between these two combatants: they agreed that the autonomy issue was of minor importance and consequently there was no reasonable argument for the voter to give political support to neither the Separatists nor the Unionists.

At the following election to the Danish Parliament eight months later the reaction came swiftly. The Separatists and the Unionists argued that the dispute between the Social Democrats and the Conservatives was in fact a farce covering up the realities. The realities being the similarities in concrete politics and not the dissimilarity between socialism and liberalism. The Separatists launched the term 'private communism' to portray the common features of the political programmes of the two parties, trying to undermine the dichotomy between left and right. Instead it emphazised the overall importance of independence from Denmark.[12]

Establishing the party system

After this introduction to the parties and the political scene of the present day, let us then return to the birth of the political party system in the Løgting. We have to do so if we want to understand the *dissimilarities* between, for instance, the Faroese party system and the Danish. It is important to emphasize this because it seems to be tempting to overlook the differences and stress the similarities. For instance, the Faroese delegates in the Nordic Council join established groups: the Conservative, the Social Democratic, the Communist or the Centre group. The fact that the Faroese

delegates in the Danish Parliament often join the correlating party groups might lead us to the same conclusion: that the party system is parallel to the party systems in the bigger Nordic countries and that the parallels are following the left/right dichotomy. The fact that major parts of fellow Nordic parties' programmes are analogous indicate the same point.

It is, nevertheless, the deviation rather than the affinity that is the main characteristic of Faroese parties during the first decades of this century. In the other Nordic countries the general tendency was that delegates chosen individually formed the first political parties from within the Parliament and so in the Løgting. But in the Løgting, which at this stage had only advisory competence, the delegates did not make right/left wings as they did abroad. Although they were familiar with this kind of grouping from their membership of the Danish Parliament, and they frequently found themselves organised as either a liberal leftist or more likely a conservative rightist when joining Danish politics, they seemed to agree in rejecting this common framework. They did form groups in the Løgting, which later became parties, but not a Left or liberal party nor a Right or conservative party. Instead of this kind of grouping they formed a *unionist* constellation and an *autonomist* constellation. It seems that they were more anxious to present general politics than being eager to represent specific class interests. It should be mentioned that some of the people behind the Autonomists had earlier run for elections with a programme containing land reforms. That was back in 1903. This fragment of a social welfare programme was neglected when the formation of the party took place six years later.[13]

It is therefore indisputable that the distinction between left and right does not make much sense. Rather, when looking at Faroese politics, we should bear in mind the other dichotomy, unionism versus autonomism.[14]

As a summary of the first decades in the history of the parties we could use this figure: *(see figure 4)*

During the year between 1906 and the interwar period there were two parties, the Autonomists and the Unionists. Not grouping horisontally, following the left/right distinction but vertically, following the dichotomy unionism/separatism. It is important to notice that at this early moment up to about 1930 you cannot talk about *absolute* separatism in Faroese politics – the debate concentrated on the *degree* of Home Rule. The Unionists at this time are a great deal more dependence-minded than the autonomists are independence-minded.

Left/right into party politics

We have to wait until the years of recession in world economics in the 1930s before it makes sense to speak

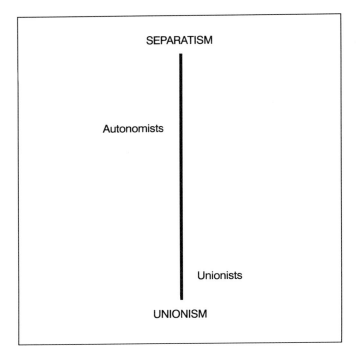

Fig. 4. The system of political parties: 1906 – interwar world crisis

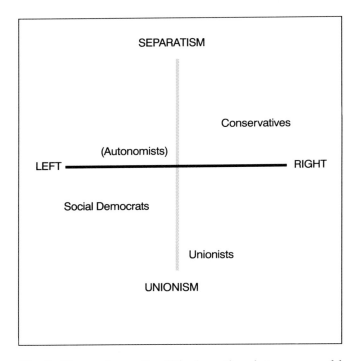

Fig. 5. The system of political parties: interwar world crisis – 1950s

of Left and Right in party politics. During the crisis two more parties are formed with the purpose of representing concrete *economic* and class interests. The Social Democrats, Javnaðarflokkurin, claims to be representing the working class. The Conservatives, first as Vinnuflokkurin, later as Fólkaflokkurin, claim to represent private business and the fishing industry.[15]

Now the party system comes to look like this: *(see figure 5).*

In this period the dichotomy between separatism and unionism is clearly subordinated to the antagonism between the left and the right. It should be noted however, that the Keynesian way of dealing with the crisis, which the Social Democrats enacted in the parliament, was a policy within a unionist context. The Conservatives, on the contrary, demanded more autonomy to be able to enact their kind of policy, a mercantilistic management of the crisis.

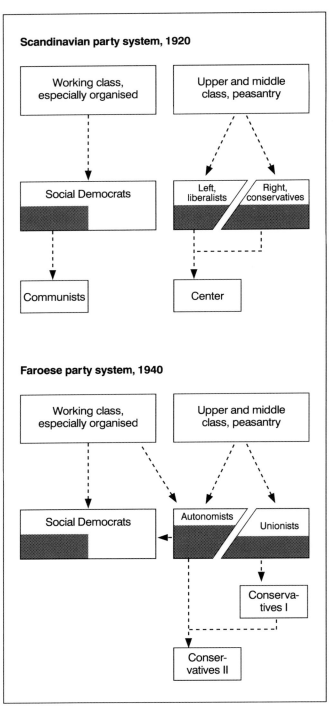

Fig. 6. The Faroese party system compared with the Scandinavian party system

Comparisons to the Scandinavian party systems

But let us save the political details for a while and sum up by comparing this party system and its development with the socalled "1920-party system" in the Scandinavian countries.[16] *(See figure 6)*

In the Scandinavian systems delegates already elected formed the first political parties – the parties usually named Left, being liberals, and Right, being conservatives.

Since its institution in the middle of the 19th century and the beginning of this century the Løgting had no legislative power, but only the right to propose legislation for approval by the Danish Parliament. The first political parties were like the Scandinavian, formed as groupings inside the Parliament – or County Council we might call it. But in contrast to the development in the Scandinavian system, the Faroese parties as mentioned were not divided into Left- and Right-parties. Instead it was the question of staying in a close union with Denmark or gaining more autonomy, which divided the members of the Løgting into two parties. The parties being Sambandsflokkurin, the Unionists, and Sjálvstýrisflokkurin, the Autonomists.[17]

In the Scandinavian party system the parties can easily be connected with social classes: the Right being the party representing the bourgeoisie, the landowners and to some extent the upper middle class in the cities, the Left especially representing the farmers and the peasants.

In the Faroes this "right/left" is a more dubious perspective. It looks as if the first parties were anxious not to be labelled agents of social classes.[18]

Unionists and Separatists in the 1930s

Among the Unionists this "no-class-politics" seems to have been a general agreement. For instance, when the party had two Faroese members in the two houses of the Danish Parliament, as it did most of the time, one went to the liberals and the other to the conservatives. Without either being more or less liberal or conservative than the other.

It was apparently a little more strenuous in the other party, the Autonomists, to create and stick to a similar consensus that it was a *populistic* party, or perhaps better, a party for all regardless of class. On the one hand its charismatic leader and one of its founders was a wealthy farmer, named *Jóannes Paturson*, from the largest of all farms of the islands. On the other hand there was a socialist wing. Some of these socialists were associated with the early Fishermen's Union, being influential members in it. The secretary of the union, *Rasmus Rasmussen*, was a member of the Løgting, representing the Autonomists. It was very clear from his writings that he was a socialist. The pre-

sident of the fishermen's union, *Símun Pauli Konoy*, on one occasion candidated outside the parties with the outspoken purpose to highlight social issues, which tended to be neglected in the tension between unionists and autonomists.[19] He claimed the counterpart to be "the smart moneymakers" at *Dimmalætting*, the Unionist paper. That was back in 1914. The president of the union was elected but almost instantly joined the Autonomists. The bourgeoisie indeed disliked events and campaigns like these. They were on the alert after this assault and surely distrusted the Autonomists.[20]

The Autonomists soon recovered their populist and popular image when a young lawyer from the most powerful dynasty, the *Mortensen-family*, joined the party. Under his leadership the populist orientation became more unambigious and sophisticated. Now the adversary was claimed to be the Danish officials, especially the autocratic Governor, blamed for his abuse of power. Formulated in this way the aim was obviously to unite all people, because almost everybody, the merchant, the shipowner, the wealthy farmer, the poor peasant, even the teacher, who denied to teach in Danish, had their quarrels with the governor.[21]

The struggle between Unionists and Autonomists nevertheless resembled the struggle abroad between the Left and the Right. In spite of the differences just mentioned the Autonomists and the liberal Left had one thing in common: they fought for extended power to the Løgting. Their opponents, the Unionists and the conservative Right, respectively, fought back trying to preserve the existing order. Both in the Scandinavian and in the Faroese party system, it was *traditionalism* against political *reformism* that was at issue in the main conflicts in the parliaments.

The incentive of the traditionalists was everywhere the wish to defend old privileges. In the Faroes it seemed very clear that resistance against the allocation of legislative powers to the Løgting, was in fact a show of defiance against income taxes. Taxes paid at this time were merely symbolic. So citizens with a substantial income were eager to prevent the Løgting from collecting tax.[22] In a way there was a connection with class interests, after all. On the other hand there were no major clashes as to the general right to vote, as it occasionally happened in neighbouring countries.

Class conflicts in interwar politics

Modern society conditioned by fishing, which took over peasant society, pushed forward new demands on the political system. Not until several decades after the foundation of trade unions in the Nordic countries, similar organisations were formed in the Faroes. The fishermen had their union founded in 1911. It was a union representing fishermen from all over the country. Four years later the first local *trade union* was founded, but ten years more had to pass until it was integrated with other local unions into a centralized organisation. This happened in 1925.

The same year the *Social Democrats* as a political party came into being. It was founded by the local unions but with a considerable support – some would say by initiative[23] – from the Danish Social Democratic Party.

Like the Social Democratic parties abroad this party was first founded outside the parliament and then had candidates elected to the Løgting. Compared to the larger Nordic countries, it never achieved the same strength. Occasionally it has been the largest party, but generally the leading 3 and later the dominating 4 have been fairly equal in strength. Therefore the Social Democrats never had the same outstanding position on the Faroes as in Scandinavia.

Ten years later *Vinnuflokkurin*, or the first *Conservative Party*, was founded. In contrast to the conservative Right in the other Nordic countries, it was first founded outside the parliament, and then later had candidates elected. Likewise its purpose was to represent private business and industry. A few years later, in 1939, the party merged with a group breaking with the Autonomists. Jóannes Patursson, aforementioned leader of the Autonomists, reacted against a social legislation including land reforms. The result of the fusion was that Fólkaflokkurin, even more than Vinnuflokkurin, resembled the Nordic conservative Right. The new party, Fólkaflokkurin, is here called the *Conservatives II*.

Thus the party system at the beginning of World War II had very much in common with the Scandinavian party system of 1920. To the left there was a big Social Democratic Party representing wage earners, to the right a Conservative Party representing private enterprise and more wealthy farmers. Somewhere in between were the Unionists not claiming to represent any particular class.

Maybe this is the main difference compared to the other Nordic countries: *there was never an agrarian party in the Faroes.* The Unionists never seemed to care enough for the peasantry to be willing to play such a part and the Autonomist party was rapidly diminishing due to the polarisation between the new Left, the Social Democrats, and the Right, the conservative Fólkaflokkurin.

Although there were a few communists critising the Social Democrats, no communist party was founded.

The struggle between autonomy and unionism had not vanished completely, though it seemed to be fading out because of the polarisation between left and right. Yet the conflict persisted within and to some extent *between* the new parties.

The Social Democrats in the Faroes had from the beginning, like the Icelandic, very close ties to the Danish Social Democrats. Therefore it was in a more influential position than the other parties when the Danish Social Democrats were in power, as they were during the thirties. But the ties caused some disagreement within the party. One question was whether the party should have a more independent and Faroese profile.[24]

About the same time there was a similar disagreement in the trade unions as to whether they should join the Danish central organisation of trade unions, the DSF.[25]

Among the Conservatives there were tensions too. On the one hand the former leader of the Autonomists, Jóannes Patursson, had become more and more a separatist. On the other hand, the original core from the first conservative party, Vinnuflokkurin, never wanted to overdo this autonomy business.

The left/right dichotomy, however, did not prevail as long as the antagonism between autonomy from and union with Denmark had done previously.

It seems to be an unstable party system along this left/right axis, the axis maybe a little wrung – the left towards unionism, the right towards autonomy.

With the German occupation of Denmark on the 9th of April 1940, and the British occupation of the Faroes three days later, all connection between Denmark and this part of the Kingdom of Denmark was severed and rendered impossible. This made a number of practical changes necessary. The executive powers were now transferred from the Danish Government to the Danish Governor of the Faroes, and a form of legislative power was transferred to the Løgting. But the Danish Governor retained the right to veto.

The postwar party system

After the war it was unthinkable that there could be a return to the constitutional status which existed prior to the war. Discussions took place at different levels, but they failed to reach an agreement on a new political setting. It was therefore decided to hold a referendum.

The referendum held in september 1946 resulted in a majority in favour of independence. But it was not a clear majority. Neither the Danish Government nor the Faroese Løgting had expected this result, so it all ended in a mess. Especially because there was no agreement whether the referendum should be considered merely as an indication of public opinion or as actually binding. The King – i.e. the Danish Government – dissolved the Løgting and demanded a new election.

This newly elected Løgting with a clear majority *against* secession continued negotiations with the Danish Government. The result was a kind of Home Rule, the Self-Government Act of 1948, which today, 1991, is still the judicial foundation both for Faroese Politics and for the relations to Denmark.

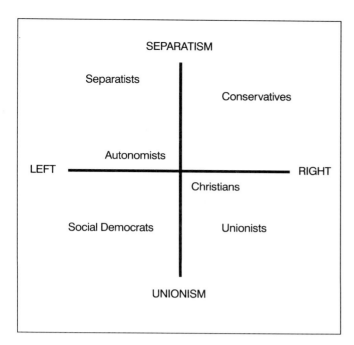

Fig. 7. The system of political parties: 1950s – present time

All this turmoil made the left/right party system of the 30s and 40s capsize. In addition to the three big parties, the Social Democrats, the Unionists, and the Conservatives, the fourth of the larger parties existing today, the *Separatists*, was founded.

The Separatists based their existence on the dissatisfaction among separatist Social Democrats and Conservatives.[26] The party apparently soon succeeded in taking over the socialist voters, who supported the Autonomists before the war. One of the party leaders became president of the Fishermen's Union. In a way the Separatists took over the Autonomist's part as a populist party although it was more radical in questions concerning the relationships with Denmark.

Now we get the situation as we know it today: *(see figure 7).*

This party system has been very stable. The four big parties have generally had each 20 to 25 per cent of the votes at elections to the Løgting.

The stable and double left/right-party system

There must be some explanation, why this party system with two dichotomies has been so stable for more than 40 years. This allegation respecting stability may have to be modified. As mentioned in the beginning there are current tendencies to place the larger parties on the axis instead of in their traditional corner positions. That, of course, will break up the picture of the party system that we have grown so used to. In a strange way this only puts the parties back to their original emphasis in the early party programmes.

The Social Democrats' first piority was from the beginning to improve conditions for the wage earners and the marginalised groups in society. In this context the constitutional links with Denmark are matters of tactics. There are several reasons why the party is not so anxious anymore to stress the unity with Denmark. The main reason is money. The conditions for carrying out welfare politics are not as good as they used to be. The Faroese government cannot rely on the Danish government to pay the extra bill as they did before. So the argument that the Faroese society was entitled to the same welfare since it was a part of the Danish society, has lost its strength. The weakened position of the Danish Social Democrats is pulling in the same direction.

The Conservatives from the very start represented business and the industry. The question concerning increased autonomy was always subordinate to this and never an end in itself. The old nationalist image has been rejected and other nationalist tendencies have developed during the last years. The new conservatism with its emphasis on a common identity for the Western communities, the Free World against communism being the real threat, paved the way for a de facto recognition of NATO military installations and presence in the Faroes. A new kind of nationalism seems nowadays to replace the other two, namely a European nationalism. Now the threat is the economic giants Japan and the United States. This new European identification tends to undermine the Faroese identity as well as replacing the Danish identity.

Separation and fishermen

The Separatist Party has always been a populist party. They put the people in focus and not some particular class. At least they do not exclude any class. Indeed it has been associated with the fishermen, but there is no contradiction in this. The party tactics are adjusted to the classes putting forward demands in favour of separatism. Which groups in society are to become the core of its voters is therefore a changing matter.

In the mid-fifties the fishermen in the Fishermen's Union formed the most nationalist group partly because of the intervention of the special labour market court in Denmark in a conflict with the shipowners. But basically it was the demands for extended fishing territories around the islands that gave strength to nationalism in this group.

In the early seventies the fishermen onboard small self-owned cutters were the group most resistant to EEC-membership. The party demanded separation and warned that the constitutional links with Denmark could become dangerous. They could very well be pulling us into the EEC together with the Danes. EEC-membership would consequently exclude Faroese control over an extended fishing territory and al-

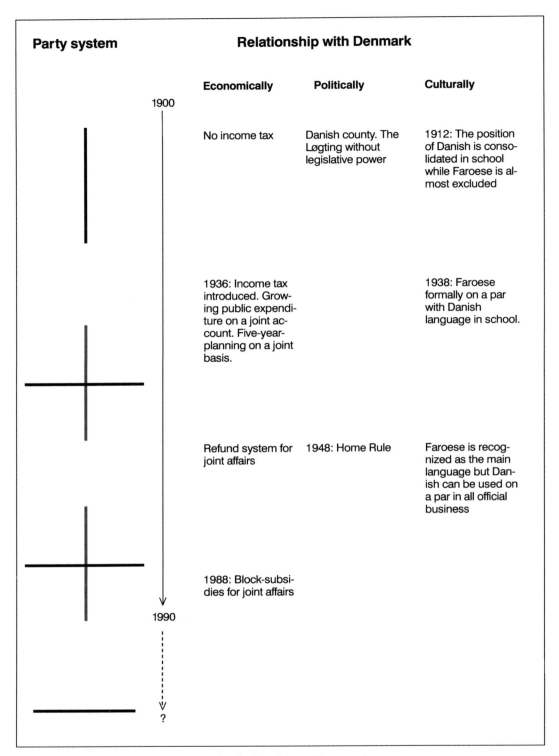

Party system	Relationship with Denmark		
	Economically	**Politically**	**Culturally**
1900			
	No income tax	Danish county. The Løgting without legislative power	1912: The position of Danish is consolidated in school while Faroese is almost excluded
	1936: Income tax introduced. Growing public expenditure on a joint account. Five-year-planning on a joint basis.		1938: Faroese formally on a par with Danish language in school.
	Refund system for joint affairs	1948: Home Rule	Faroese is recognized as the main language but Danish can be used on a par in all official business
	1988: Block-subsidies for joint affairs		
1990			
?			

Fig. 8. Changes in party system and relationship to Denmark

low British and German trawlers to continue fishing the stocks that the inshore fishermen wanted so dearly.

Today the party is in a classless position so to speak, trying to compensate its losses with a more populistic rhetoric. Compared to the Social Democrats its position towards the unions is much weaker.

Unionists, lower taxation and Danish subsidies

In a similar way we have a populist party, the Unionists, struggling for unity with Denmark. Their main objection to autonomy is that autonomy means more tax on the Faroese. The party has an easier task than the Separatists, because it does not have to change its social base from time to time. It can rely on the simple fact that all citzens are against higher taxes.

It is tempting to say that the parties polarising along the separatism/unionism axis are parties that put emphasis on presenting politics. And that the parties along the left/right axis are parties accentuating their role as representing the working class and the industry, respectively.

This way of perceiving politics would fit well into a most common comprehension: that the question of left or right is about economy, whereas the other dichotomy has to do with culture and mere politics. – This perception is not very illuminating, however.

The quarrels as to the union with Denmark have always been basically economic, and in fact most of the time about Danish money, – Danish state subsidies, direct or indirect. The real and serious debate has never been about Faroese resources being transferred to the Danish empire, as the colonial position might indicate to foreigners.

There seems to be a correlation between the set-up of the political party system and the way the Danish money is flowing into the islands.

The foundation of the Unionist Party was first of all a reaction against a proposal that the Løgting be given legislative powers in fields of activities supported economically by the Faroes themselves. This would imply the introduction of income tax and concomitant redistribution of economic assests in Faroese society. The Unionists reacted very sharply first of all on behalf of the wealthy officials, farmers and shipowners.[27].

So in a way the Unionist Party was a rightist reaction more than anything else. Danish patriotism among Faroese did not reach ecstatic heights until the crucial proposal had been rejected. Because of money, the *cultural nationalism* that had existed for a while, suddenly became a political issue. The Unionists subsequently overdid things in order to prove their Danish loyalties. The most critical part of this proces was the consolidation of the Danish language in the schools in a position it had never had before, at the same time pushing Faroese language and culture into a marginal position.[28] This can hardly be seen as anything but giving a profitable political system legitimacy.

This was the situation until the thirties, when the Social Democrats strengthened their position in the Løgting. In Denmark a Social Democrat, Stauning, was Prime Minister, thus paving the way for a Faroese – and Danish – discussion as to who was to benefit from the money Denmark paid to governmental activities in the islands. In this way the left/right dimension was strengthened within the Løgting.

In the mid-thirties the Danish government enforced the proposal that the Faroese should pay income tax to contribute their share of the growing expenditure – expenditures that were due to costly Keynesian intervention to help the economy through the crisis.

Now the political scene was accessible for left/right struggle on economic values created in the Faroes.[29] As a consequence of this the Conservatives were founded.

Subsidies to trawlers or employment – Danish and Faroese tax money

The struggle between the Conservatives and Social Democrats resembles the political debate today, the issues being whether tax money is to be given out as subsidies to the trawlers or to public employment. Related to this is the question of how to deal with the tax assessment. At the same time a new dimension has been introduced by the fact that governmental expenditures are financed not only by the State – but from now on also by Faroese tax payers.

The division in tax collecting was refined in the Self-Government Act which also divided the administrative areas in two categories mainly corresponding to the double tax collecting. The Løgting got control of legislation and administration of some areas, on the exclusive terms that the Faroese should then have to pay by themselves.

If we look at the welfare politics of the two larger leftist parties, the main difference between the Social Democrats and the Separatists is, *who is to pay the bill.*[30] The Social Democrats see the Faroese as a part of Danish society. The constitutional links, they used to claim, implicate that the standard of living should be the same in Denmark and the Faroes. The best and most well-known example is the law on retirement pension from 1958. As a matter of fact it was the Danish law from 1957 which was made Faroese. There was a difference, however. The Danes are paying to both, whereas the Faroese pay only a part of the Faroese retirement pension.[31]

In contrast, proposals by the Separatists are generally based on Faroese tax incomes. This doubling in governmental financing creates the basis for a double party system, so to speak. Two parties to the left and two parties to the right.

Recently this has been changed. Again following a Danish initiative and pressure on the Løgting. Formerly the Danish State paid a certain part, a percentage, of different expenditures. It was a highly complex system but the result was that when the Faroese decided to expand the expenditures, a proportionate increase in subsidies was released.

This was changed in 1988.

The Faroese government is now receiving an absolute amount of unspecified subsidies from the State. Then the Løgting must decide how to spend this amount.

Outlook

This system of state subsidizing can be expected to enhance prospects of conflict along the left/right axis, as resources coming from Denmark are no longer earmarked. At the same time it is weakening the separatism/unionism dimension in Faroese politics.

So a plausible future organisation within Faroese parliamentary politics could be the following:

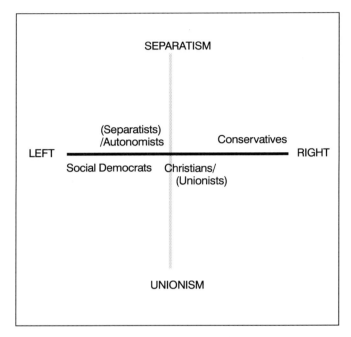

Fig. 9. The system of political parties: in the future?

The tendencies outlined might be reinforced by current tendencies of another kind in Western Europe: the left-wing parties have generally been forced to broaden their electoral appeal to meet the decline in the social base. In countries with sentiments for regionalist and peripheral nationalism this has included a more explicit territorial dimension[32] in public politics.

The transition to block-subsidies from the Danish state is somehow outdating the Self-Government Act, because it undermines the division of legislative and administrative areas which has existed until now. It puts the Social Democratic Party – and not the Separatists – into a favourable position, because the Social Democrats can benefit from regionalist sentiment by offering a combination of limited territorial autonomy, regional defence within the institutions of the existing State and a guarantee against separatism. As a peripheral nationalist party the Separatists are able to offer only the former, thus limiting their appeal.

This process is likely to become very complicated as Denmark is going on integrating politically into the European Community, while the Faroes prefer to stay outside.

Notes

1. This article is a slightly revised version of a lecture given on October 24, 1990 at the symposium "Local organization, cultural identity and national integration in the North Atlantic and the Arctic" at the Center for North Atlantic Studies, University of Aarhus October 22-24, 1990.
2. For instance Zakarias Wang 1968: 104 ff; Zakarias Wang 1988: 149; Kurt Johannesen 1980: 52 and Kristian á Neystabø 1984: 22.
3. Ingemar Lindblad et. al. 1984: 92.
4. This perspective is especially acknowledged in Stein Rokkans theoretical achievements. For instance Stein Rokkan and Derek Urwin 1982 and 1983.
5. Often referred to as the Home Rule Party.
6. Often referred to as the People's Party.
7. Often referred to as the Republican Party.
8. At full length its name is the Christian People's Party/Progress and Fisheries Party.
9. At full length its name is the Socialist Secession Party.
10. Wang, Johannesen and Neystabø, op. cit.
11. The Faroese elect 2 out of 179 members of the Danish Parliament.
12. Andras Róin makes a point of a similar tendency among party voters regarding ideological attitudes, Róin 1988: 94.
13. Jóannes Dalsgaard 1971: 39.
14. Róland Waag Høgnesen 1968: 74.
15. Róland Waag Høgnesen op. cit., Zakarias Wang 1968: 82.
16. The figure "The Scandinavian party system, 1920" is from the book *Politik i Norden* by Ingemar Lindblad et.al., Lindblad 1984: 69.
17. Zakarias Wang 1968: 79 ff.
18. Jóannes Dalsgaard op. cit.
19. Jóannes Dalsgaard 1971: 45
20. Jóannes Dalsgaard 1971: 112 ff.
21. Jóannes Dalsgaard 1971: 130 ff.
22. Róland Waag Høgnesen 1968: 79, Hans Jacob Debes 1982:
23. Zakarias Wang 1968: 80.
24. A very interesting and illuminating debate on the issue is found in the party paper, *Færøernes Socialdemokrat,* July 1928.
25. Tórður Jóansson 1975: 94 ff.
26. Zakarias Wang 1988: 144.
27. Hans Jacob Debes 1982:
28. Jørgen-Frantz Jacobsen 1927: 66; Arnfinnur Thomassen 1985: 49ff.
29. In addition to income tax there were duties. It should be noted, however, that income tax in the Faroes was still of minor importance compared to especially export duty.
30. Beinta í Jákupsstovu 1982: 75.
31. Beinta í Jákupsstovu 1982: 67ff.
32. Michael Keating 1988: 238ff.

References

Dalsgaard, Jóannes 1971. *De færøske partier og deres stilling til forholdet mellem Færøerne og det danske rige 1906-1916.* University of Copenhagen.

Debes, Hans Jacob 1982. *Nú er tann stundin...: Tjóðskaparrørsla og sjálvstýrispolitikkur til 1906 – við søguligum baksýni.* Tórshavn: Føroya Skúlabókagrunnur.

Færøernes Socialdemokrat 1928. (Party Paper).

Høgnesen, Róland Waag 1968. "Færøernes historie frem til den anden verdenskrig". In: *Færinger-Frænder: Sprog, historie, politik og økonomi.* Edited by Anders Ølgaard, pp. 43-75. Copenhagen: Gyldendal.

Jacobsen, Jørgen-Frantz 1927. *Danmark og Færøerne.* København.

Jákupsstovu, Beinta í 1982. *Heimestyreordninga og sosialpolitikk på Færøyane.* University of Bergen.

Jóansson, Tórður 1975. *Saman tí standið: Fimti ára minningarrit Føroya Arbeiðarafelags.* Tórshavn: Føroya Arbeiðarafelag.

Johannesen, Kurt 1980. *Færøsk fiskeri- og markedspolitik i 70'erne.* Århus Universitet.

Keating, Michael 1988. *State and regional nationalism: Territorial politics and the European state.* London. Harvester-Wheatsheaf.

Lindblad, Ingemar et. al 1984. *Politik i Norden: En jamförande over-sikt.* Stockholm: Liber Forlag.

Neystabø, Kristian á 1984. *Færøerne og EF.* Tórshavn: Egií forlag.

Róin, Andras 1988. *Færøske lagtingsvalg: En analyse, der fokuserer på vælgeradfærden og det todimensionelle partisystem.* University of Aarhus.

Rokkan, Stein and Derek W. Urwin 1983. *Economy, Territory, Ident-ity: Politics of West European Peripheries.* London: Sage.

1982. *The Politics of Territorial Identity: Studies in European regio-nalism.* London: Sage.

Thomassen, Arnfinnur 1985. *Færøsk i den færøske skole: Fra århun-dredskiftet til 1938.* Odense Universitet.

Wang, Zakarias 1968. "Færøsk politik i nyere tid". In: *Færinger-Frænder: Sprog, historie, politik og økonomi.* Edited by Anders Øl-gaard, pp. 76-110. Copenhagen: Gyldendal.

1988. *Stjórnmálafrøði.* Hoyvík: Futura.

The Authors

Bjørklund, Ivar. Social anthropologist, lecturer at Tromsø Museum. Currently research associate at the social science institute, Tromsø University. Fields of research: ethnicity and resource management in northern Norway. Address: Institutt for Museumsvirksomhet, Samisk-etnografisk avdeling, Folkeparken, N-9000 Tromsø, Norway. Tel: +47 083 45 000; Fax: +47 083 80 836.

Dorais, Louis-Jacques, b. 1945. Anthropologist, professor at Université Laval, Québec, since 1972. Fields of research: Inuit language, society and identity; social organisation of the Vietnamese immigrants and refugees in Canada. Publications: *Inuit Languages and Dialects* (1990); *Exile in a Cold Land. A Vietnamese Community in Canada* (1987). Address: Département d'anthropologie, Université Laval, Québec, Canada, G1K 7P4. Tel: +1 418 656 7827; Fax: +1 418 656 2831.

Dybbroe, Susanne , b. 1951. Social anthropologist, lecturer in anthropology at Aarhus University since 1987. Regional specialisation and area of field research, Greenland. Focus of research interest: gender, culture and development and related issues of identity in the Arctic and in comparative perspective. The author of a number of articles in this field, e.g. "Participation and control: issues in the debate on women and development – a Greenlandic example" (1988); "Questions of identity and issues of self-determination" (1990). Address: Dept. of Social Anthropology, Aarhus University, Moesgård, DK-8270 Højbjerg, Denmark. Tel: +45 86 272433; Fax: +45 86 272378.

Jenkins, Richard. Social anthropologist, senior lecturer in sociology at University College, Swansea, Wales. Has carried out research in Northern Ireland, the West Midlands region of England and South Wales. Currently engaged with Dr. C. Davies on a study of young people with learning disabilities. The author of *Lads, Citizens, and ordinary Kids* (1983); *Racism and Recruitment* (1986); *Taking the Strain* (with S. Hutson, 1989); *The Myth of the Hidden Economy* (with P. Harding, 1989); *Pierre Bourdieu* (forthcoming). Address: Dept. of Sociology and Social Anthropology, University College, Singleton Park, Swansea SA2 8PP, Wales. Tel: +44 0792 295309; Fax: +44 0792 295750.

Mørkøre, Jógvan. Cand. polit. from the University of Copenhagen, lecturer in the social science dept. at the University of the Faroes. Fields of research: political institutions and resource management in the Faroe Islands. Address: Samfelagsvísindi, Fróðskaparsetur Føroya, Nóatún, FR-100 Tórshavn, Faroe Islands. Tel: +298 1 88 91; Fax: +298 1 68 44.

Stordahl, Vigdis. Cand. polit. from Tromsø University 1982. Currently engaged at the regional centre in northern Norway for child and youth psychiatry in the development of a culturally sensitive approach in psychiatric diagnostics and treatment. Has previously worked on Sami interest organisations and models of self-government for indigeneous peoples. Address: Regionsenteret for barne- og ungdomspsykiatri, Kautokeino, Norway.

Thuesen, Søren Thue, b. 1958. BA in Greenland studies, 1981, and MA in history of literature, 1986, from Aarhus University. 1987-88 & 1989-91 research associate of CNS, Aarhus, resp. Institute of Eskimology, University of Copenhagen. 1988-89 lecturer at the Greenlandic university, Ilisimatusarfik, where he taught literature. Field of research: national Greenlandic culture and institutions in the 19th and 20th centuries. The author of *Fremad, opad. Kampen for en moderne grønlandsk identitet* /'The struggle for a modern Greenlandic identity'/ (1988). Address: Lyngbyvej 32 F, DK-2100 København Ø, Denmark.